Guide to The National Museum of Ethnology

Note: Japanese is romanized according to the Kunrei system, except for authors' names, which follow personal preferences.

This edition is based on a translation of the Japanese edition of the catalogue, originally published in 1986. English-language editorial consultant: Optima Co., Ltd.

Produced by Kodansha Ltd., 12-21 Otowa 2-chome, Bunkyo-ku, Tokyo 112, Japan.
Edited and published by the National Museum of Ethnology, 10-1 Senri Expo Park, Suita, Osaka 565, Japan.
Copyright © 1991 by the National Museum of Ethnology, 10-1 Senri Expo Park, Suita, Osaka 565, Japan. All rights reserved. Printed in Japan.
ISBN 4-06-204846-9
First edition, 1991

Contents

An aerial view of the National Museum of Ethnology, which was designed by Kisho Kurokawa.

Preface

Ethnology, or cultural anthropology, is the comparative study of societies and cultures throughout the world, and thus the National Museum of Ethnology is dedicated to the cultures of the peoples of the world. Similar museums were established in Europe and North and South America more than half a century ago; in Japan, however, although such a museum was planned over fifty years ago, it was only established as recently as 1974, and the exhibitions were finally opened to the public in November 1977. Nevertheless, in size and conception, our museum ranks among the leaders of its kind.

The National Museum of Ethnology is both a museum and a research institute for ethnological studies, one of the Inter-University Research Institutes. Over sixty staff members engaged in ethnological research are continually bringing back new artifacts for the museum, and the results of their research are constantly being incorporated in the displays. Research is also being pursued in conjunction with scholars at universities all over Japan. In April 1989, the School of Cultural Studies was established in the museum as one part of the Graduate University for Advanced Studies.

It is one of the museum's chief aims to make the exhibits understandable not only to experts but also to the general public. We sincerely hope this guide will enable visitors to gain a deeper comprehension of both the culture of peoples around the globe and Japanese culture by showing the similarities and contrasts between Japanese and other cultures.

TADAO UMESAO
Director-General

An Introduction to the Exhibits

The museum presents the cultures and lifestyles of peoples throughout the world from the viewpoint of ethnology, or cultural anthropology. While artifacts are displayed in isolation in most conventional museums, this does not allow visitors to understand the culture of a region. In the National Museum of Ethnology, however, related artifacts are grouped together to show in an effective manner the ways of life of each people.

To achieve this, project teams were first formed from our research staff to establish the main themes for each region. For instance, the Oceania exhibit—the first one the visitor encounters—presents the following four themes: the seafaring peoples of Oceania, their lifestyles, the world of rituals, and the Australian Aborigines. Each theme may also be divided into subthemes, depending on the artifacts on display, and it is not unjustified to claim that our displays enable visitors to "read" the culture and lifestyles of the various peoples. We have avoided rigidly keeping to the same concepts in each region, since we hope to help visitors realize the cultural diversity of the world's peoples.

All cultures are treated equally by the museum, since our policy is to regard cultural differences as exemplifying the wealth of cultural diversity rather than to judge them in terms of superiority or inferiority. Hence, regional exhibits are not organized according to national boundaries but according to ecological or geographical groups, and cultural groups. These classifications may be changed in the future as research advances.

The Exhibits

The museum features two types of exhibitions—permanent exhibits and special exhibits. The former may be classified as either regional or cross-cultural exhibits, while the latter are organized under various themes several times a year. At present, regional exhibits are classified according to area: Oceania, the Americas, Europe, Africa, West Asia, Southeast Asia, Central and North Asia, and East Asia. As the exhibition halls are expanded, other regional exhibits will be added to the existing ones. Cross-cultural exhibits deal with music and languages from a global point of view, and more themes of this kind will be presented as artifacts are collected.

At present (as of January 1991), only about 5 percent of the museum's collection, or 9,030 items, is on permanent display, while the remaining 176,000 items are stored for research purposes. Most of the objects on display are not old, but instead they embody a region's ethnic cultural tradition and are still in use today.

The Exhibition Rooms

The permanent exhibition comprises six rooms or halls, which may be extended when necessary. At the center of each room is a 20-square-meter patio specially designed to introduce natural lighting into the exhibition rooms, to function as symbolic space, and to display objects that are very large or are better suited for exhibition in the open air. The displays mainly consist of artifacts, with the accompanying information and illustrations presented on panels. Audio-visual material is available in the Videotheque, which might be called an additional "audio-visual exhibit."

The Videotheque, a system developed by the museum, provides an audio-visual presentation of artifacts, and visitors are free to select whatever programs they wish to see by touching directions displayed on the monitors in the viewing booths. The purpose of the Videotheque is to complement the limited explanations that accompany the artifacts in regional and cross-cultural exhibits by giving visitors a better understanding of their dynamic cultural backgrounds.

Special displays are contained in a separate 40-square-meter building that has a cylindrical central part 34 meters in diameter open from the first to the third floors, allowing artifacts up to 13 meters tall to be exhibited. The building is also equipped with the latest audio-visual equipment and computers to provide the newest type of presentation.

	Exhibition area (m²)	Number of artifacts	Number of panels
Oceania	617	722	60
The Americas	286	416	53
Europe	223	210	8
Africa	584	900	26
West Asia	296	371	11
Music	407	229	194
Language	274	58	6
Southeast Asia	637	955	74
Central and North Asia	721	744	37
East Asia			
Korea	309	425	37
China	646	773	8
The Ainu	332	537	16
Japan	1558	2690	197
Total	6890	9030	727

As of April, 1990

The Cultures of Oceania

Oceania is a world of the sea. Successive waves of migration since the Stone Age have resulted in a vast cultural continuum stretching across the islands of the Pacific Ocean. However, regional cultural variations also evolved. The everyday tools used on these resource-poor islands are embodiments of the people's lives, and the striking designs of their masks and images reveal how these island peoples viewed the world around them.

Oceania spans the vast Pacific Ocean and includes the world's smallest continent—Australia—and the world's second largest island—New Guinea—as well as some 10,000 smaller islands. Among the approximately 28 million people of Oceania, those with the oldest culture are the Aborigines of Australia, who migrated from Asia in the Upper Pleistocene period more than 50,000 years ago, when Australia was still situated near the Asian landmass. These Aborigines live by hunting and gathering using Stone Age technology and are classified as an Australoid people, with dark brown skin, broad noses, and curly hair.

More than 5,000 years ago, another great wave of migration from the Asian mainland and Southeast Asia took place, this time of Austronesian-speaking Mongoloid peoples, who have light brown skin and straight hair. Austronesian languages are spoken today primarily in Malaysia, Indonesia, and the Philippines, but they also occur in Taiwan and throughout most of Oceania and are even found across the Indian Ocean in Madagascar. These Austronesian peoples have been aptly called the "Vikings of the Pacific."

These great migrations took place long before European explorers "discovered" the islands of Oceania. The Mongoloid newcomers mixed with the original Australoid inhabitants, resulting in what are now known as the peoples of Melanesia. The inhabitants of inland New Guinea have curly hair and aquiline noses, while the people of other islands have hair ranging from curly to very curly and have conspicuously broad noses. Farthest to the east we find the Polynesians, who have some Mongoloid physical characteristics but are strikingly Melanesian in general appearance.

In the New Guinea highlands, a Neolithic level of technology, characterized by the use of stone axes and knives, was evident until quite recently. Sweet potatoes, the present staple, came from Indonesia in the fifteenth or sixteenth century and replaced taros, which, according to archaeological evidence, had been cultivated in this area for 10,000 years. Comparative linguistic evidence indicates that before their migration from Asia, the Austronesian peoples cultivated rice and raised chickens, pigs, and dogs, in addition to growing taros, yams, breadfruit, and other crops important in Oceania.

The great migrations were made possible by the development of the double canoe and the outrigger canoe, which were equipped with sails, and the magnificent navigational skills of these people have been passed down to present-day Polynesians and Micronesians. Whereas taros and breadfruit were the most important crops in the islands of Polynesia and Micronesia, in the course of adapting to the natural environment the sago palm became the staple food in the lowland areas of islands of New Guinea and Melanesia. The first section of the Oceania exhibit, which also embodies its primary theme, is "Seafaring Peoples," showing the special characteristics of the canoes, nautical charts, and fishing equipment of these seafarers.

The areas of Melanesia, Polynesia, and Micronesia (denoting "black islands," "many islands," and "small islands," respectively) are geographically and anthropologically distinct. In New Guinea and Melanesia, hereditary succession to tribal leadership did not develop, and the village remained the largest political unit. Furthermore, as belief in the supernatural power residing in humans and objects, called *mana*, and the rituals accompanying it became more elaborate, great numbers of masks and images symbolizing ancestral and other spirits were produced. In Polynesia and Micronesia, social classes developed, particularly in the former, where political systems such as kingdoms and chiefdoms appeared. Moreover, persons of high social rank who regulated behavior came to be regarded as *tapu*—a word that subsequently made its way into the English language as "taboo."

The second main theme of the Oceania exhibit concerns various characteristics of society in Oceania. Thus, the "World of Ritual" display examines Oceanic society through its masks and images. Linking "Seafaring Peoples" and "World of Ritual" is the "Daily Life in Oceania" display, which presents the third theme of the Oceania exhibit—the

Making copra, or dried coconut meat (Rabaul).

tools used in obtaining the necessities of everyday life. In addition, there is an exhibit of artifacts of the Aborigines in the Australian continent.

In modern times, most Oceanian peoples came under colonial rule, with the result that their traditional culture has rapidly disappeared. Its peoples are now caught between the demands of tradition and those of the modern world. However, as shown by the more than ten nations in the region that have recently declared independence, the peoples of Oceania are taking greater control of their own destinies. (Osamu Sakiyama)

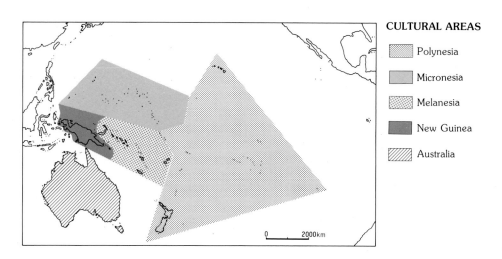

CULTURAL AREAS

- Polynesia
- Micronesia
- Melanesia
- New Guinea
- Australia

0   2000km

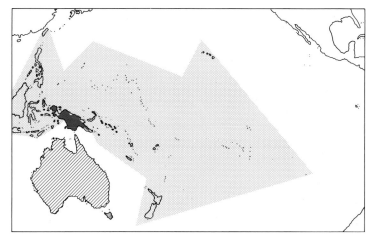

LANGUAGE DISTRIBUTION

- Austronesian Languages
- Papuan Languages
- Australian Languages
- Tasmanian Languages (extinct)

Note: The Tasmanian languages are all extinct, and in Australia, New Zealand, and Hawaii, English is now the predominant language, replacing the respective indigenous languages.

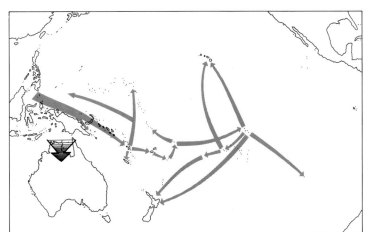

MIGRATION ROUTES

- First wave or Paleolithic migration
- Migrations since Neolithic times

Seafaring Peoples

The Pacific Ocean is dotted with some 10,000 islands, the settlement of which began in prehistoric times. Unlike the migrations on the Asian continent, those in Oceania were accomplished with great difficulty because they required navigating across thousands of kilometers of ocean. Lacking the magnetic compass and the sextant, the ancient navigators relied on indigenous skills based on their extensive knowledge of the ocean and of astronomy. For these ocean voyages, they built outrigger canoes and double canoes with two hulls. These boats are remarkable for their speed and stability. With their excellent navigational knowledge and canoes, the peoples of Oceania were able to cross the roughest seas and distinguished themselves as the greatest long-distance navigators of the ancient world. Living off the bounty of the sea, these peoples brought into being the highly complex oceanic cultures found throughout the vast Pacific region.

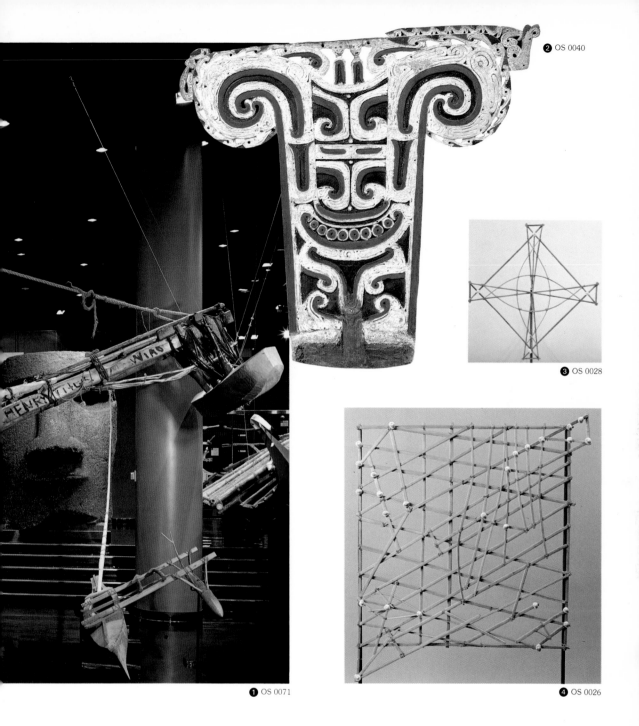

❸ OS 0028

❶ OS 0071

❹ OS 0026

❶ **Ocean-going Canoe** (Satawal Island, Micronesia). A sail-rigged outrigger of the type used for interisland voyages and for fishing expeditions. The bow, stern, and side planks are attached to a dugout lower hull with coconut sennit. This canoe normally carries a crew of eight and can reach a speed of seven knots. It successfully completed a 3,000-kilometer voyage from Satawal Island to the 1975 International Ocean Exposition held in Okinawa.

❷ **Canoe Splashboard** (Trobriand Islands, Melanesia) Affixed to bow and stern of canoes used in *kula* trading—interisland trading of such items as shell armlets and necklaces—and engraved with such images as ocean-

traversing butterflies, snakes, constellations, and guardian deities, these boards embodied prayers for a safe voyage and protection from malevolent sea spirits.

❸-❹ **Navigation Charts** (replicas) (Marshall Islands, Micronesia)
Made of coconut frond stems (showing the directions of currents) and cowrie shells (indicating the location of islands), such charts were used only for instruction and were not taken on actual voyages.

❶ OS 0041–0068

❶ **Paddles**
Paddles, poles, and rudders are indispensable to canoes, which are essential for trade and transportation in Oceania. The blades have carved designs, and some shafts have images of human faces or of half-bird, half-human figures.

❷ **Canoe Bailer** (New Zealand, Polynesia)
An elaborately carved tool for bailing water out of a canoe.

❸ **Fishing Equipment**
A selection of fishing gear used in traditional fishing techniques in Oceania. Methods include angling techniques using pole-and-line, bottom line, and troll line (using lures); net techniques using hand net, scoop net, cast net, drive-in net, and gill net; and numerous other techniques such as trapping fish, spearfishing, harpooning, diving, kite-fishing, fishing by torchlight, and the use of shark snares and stone weirs. The equipment shows the ingenious use of such simple materials as plants, shells,

❷ OS 0035

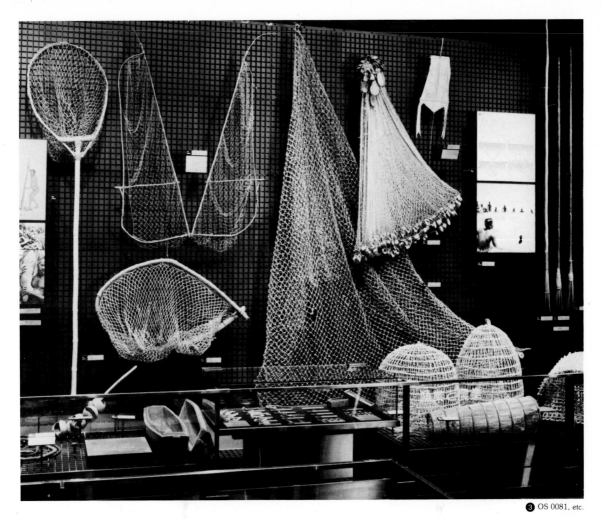

❸ OS 0081, etc.

❹ OS 0100

❻ OS 0145·0121·0127
(from left)

❺ OS 0103·0109

bones, and stones in traditional fishing technology among Oceanic peoples.

❹ **Octopus Lure** (Tonga Islands, Polynesia)

In one legend, the octopus and the rat are enemies, and, in an allusion to that, this lure is fashioned in the shape of a rat.

❺ **Lures** (*left*: Marshall Islands, Micronesia; *right*: Pohnpei Island, Micronesia)

Used for tuna and bonito fishing, the shafts of these are made of mother-of-pearl, and the hooks of turtle shell or other kinds of shell are attached with coconut palm or hibiscus fiber.

❻ **Fishhooks** (*from left*: New Zealand, Polynesia; Hawaiian Islands, Polynesia; Palau Islands, Micronesia)

Made of such materials as giant clam shell, mother-of-pearl, turtle shell, human and bird bones, stone, and wood, these are selected according to the type, size, and habits of the fish.

① OS 0250

② OS 0251

③ OS 0207

Daily Life in Oceania

The peoples of Oceania live in a variety of natural environments, from the deserts of Australia to the lush green forests of New Zealand and Melanesia, and the minute islands of Micronesia and Polynesia. However, the variety of plant and animal life is limited, and the islands are poor in food sources. This has been overcome by the ingenuity of the people: taros and sago are the staple foods in swampy areas, and yams, breadfruit, and coconuts are cultivated in drier areas. Lacking metals, Oceanian peoples fashioned their tools from available materials: axe blades were made of both stone and the thick shells of giant clams. The stone axe was extremely versatile and used for everything from felling trees and hollowing out wooden bowls and canoe hulls to carving works of art. In Melanesia, a wide variety of pottery was made for both storage and cooking. The technique of weaving on looms was unknown in Oceania, except on some islands in Micronesia, and *tapa* cloth was made from the bark fibers of the paper mulberry tree. Basket-weaving and plaiting coconut palm or pandanus leaves for floor coverings were common in Oceania. Earthen-floored houses were found everywhere, except in one small area of Melanesia and New Guinea, where houses were built on stilts.

④ OS 0139

⑤ OS 0171

⑥ OS 0159

⑧ OS 0222

⑦ OS 0249·0242

❶ Food Storage Vessel (East Sepik Province, New Guinea)
Used for storing sago palm starch, the staple food. Paint was applied after the pot was fired.

❷ Box for Valuables (New Zealand, Polynesia)
The entire surface of this box for such valuables as body ornaments is elaborately carved.

❸ Lime Holder and Spatula (East Sepik Province, New Guinea)
Made from a gourd, this container for the lime used in betel-chewing has a bone stopper that doubles as a spatula.

❹ Kava Bowl (Tonga Islands, Polynesia)
On many Pacific islands, the smashed root of the *kava* plant of the pepper family is mixed with water in a large bowl like this one and drunk ritually.

❺ Wooden Bowl (Morobe Province, New Guinea)

This type of bowl for serving food was an important trading commodity. The design represents a bird in flight, clutching a fish in its claws.

❻ Turtle-shell Tray (Palau Islands, Micronesia)
Highly valued and used as currency in ritual trade, as was bead-money.

❼ Mortar and Stone Pounder for Making Poi (Hawaiian Islands, Polynesia; Truk Islands, Micronesia)
A typical Oceanic cooking utensil, with the mortar made from a thick piece of wood and the pounder of stone or coral. To make *poi*, taros or breadfruit are cooked in an earth oven using heated stones and then pounded into a paste and flavored with coconut milk.

❽ Coconut Grater (Palau Islands, Micronesia)
The shell, or sometimes metal, blade is used to grate the meat of ripe coconuts that have been split in half, and the grated coconut is then squeezed for its milk.

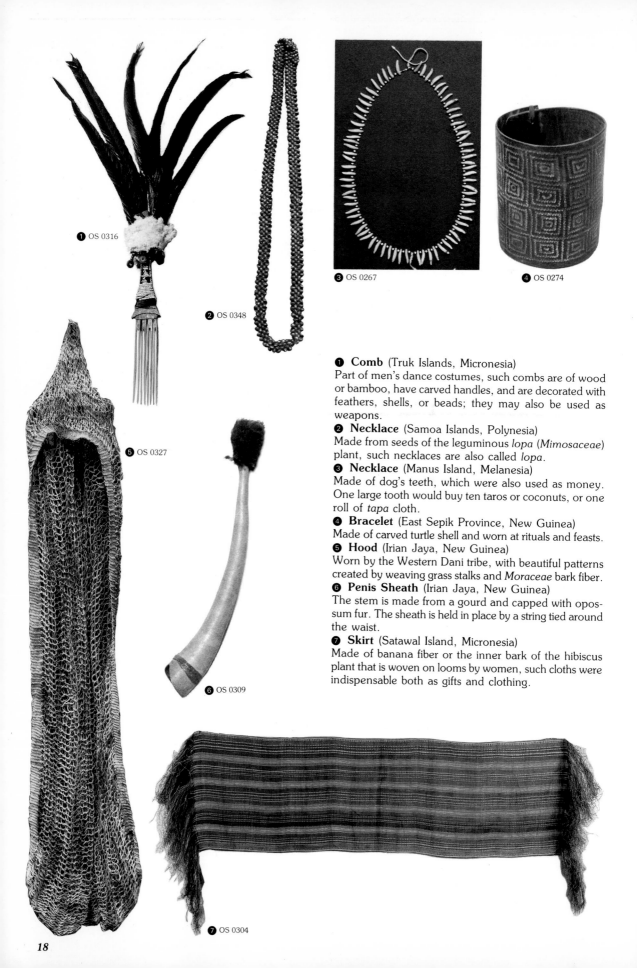

1 OS 0316

2 OS 0348

3 OS 0267

4 OS 0274

5 OS 0327

6 OS 0309

7 OS 0304

❶ Comb (Truk Islands, Micronesia)
Part of men's dance costumes, such combs are of wood or bamboo, have carved handles, and are decorated with feathers, shells, or beads; they may also be used as weapons.

❷ Necklace (Samoa Islands, Polynesia)
Made from seeds of the leguminous *lopa* (*Mimosaceae*) plant, such necklaces are also called *lopa*.

❸ Necklace (Manus Island, Melanesia)
Made of dog's teeth, which were also used as money. One large tooth would buy ten taros or coconuts, or one roll of *tapa* cloth.

❹ Bracelet (East Sepik Province, New Guinea)
Made of carved turtle shell and worn at rituals and feasts.

❺ Hood (Irian Jaya, New Guinea)
Worn by the Western Dani tribe, with beautiful patterns created by weaving grass stalks and *Moraceae* bark fiber.

❻ Penis Sheath (Irian Jaya, New Guinea)
The stem is made from a gourd and capped with opossum fur. The sheath is held in place by a string tied around the waist.

❼ Skirt (Satawal Island, Micronesia)
Made of banana fiber or the inner bark of the hibiscus plant that is woven on looms by women, such cloths were indispensable both as gifts and clothing.

8 OS 0440–OS 0467

9 OS 0474

10 OS 0408

11 OS 0410

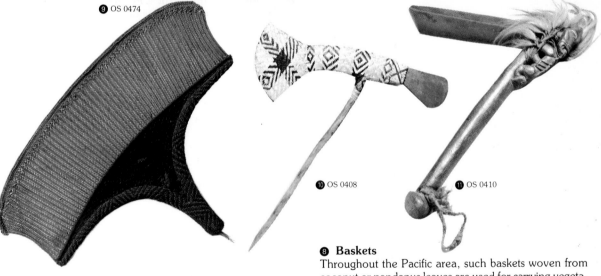

12 OS 0423

❽ Baskets
Throughout the Pacific area, such baskets woven from coconut or pandanus leaves are used for carrying vegetables, fish, and the like.

❾ Fan (Hawaiian Islands, Polynesia)
In the days of the Kamehameha kingdom, this fan of woven palm leaves was a symbol of the authority of the king. The handle is made of human hair and palm leaves.

❿ Ceremonial Stone Axe (Western Highlands Province, New Guinea)
Often used in bride-price payments. The head is attached to a thin wooden handle, then covered with woven rattan.

⓫ Ceremonial Stone Axe (New Zealand, Polynesia)
Only the Maori nobility were allowed to own such an adze-type blade of greenstone with feather decoration.

⓬ Fly Whisk (Samoa Islands, Polynesia)
Used as a symbol of authority by heads of large households on such occasions as giving a speech at the local community house.

❶ OS 0262

❷ OS 0712

❸ OS 0716

❹ OS 0723

❶ Tapa Cloth (Tonga Islands, Polynesia)
The inner bark of the paper mulberry tree was first soaked in water and pounded flat, then folded over and again pounded. The finished product, formerly used for clothing, was then stencil-dyed.
❷ Feather Money (Santa Cruz Islands, Melanesia)
Made with the feathers of three hundred birds, mainly honey-eaters, this was used for bride-price payments, and no man could marry without one.
❸ Shell Money (Yap Islands, Micronesia)
Made of black-lip shells, such money had no great value but was used as a gift in rites of passage ceremonies, or as a token of good will when seeking large favors.

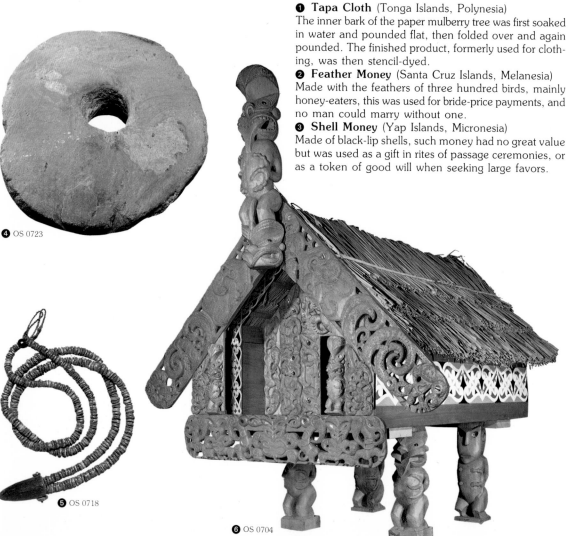

❺ OS 0718

❻ OS 0704

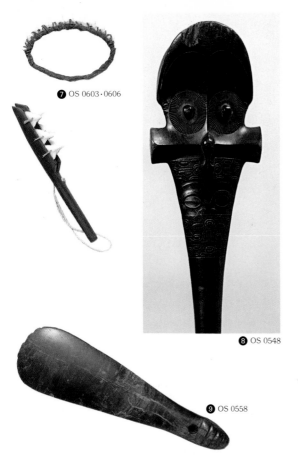

⓿ OS 0603・0606

❼ OS 0548

❾ OS 0558

❿ OS 0553

❹ Stone Money (Yap Islands, Micronesia)
Made of calcite, this is the largest currency in the world, and its value is determined by both the size and history of each stone. It was used as remuneration for the construction of a house and as part of dowries.

❺ Shell Money (Yap Islands, Micronesia)
Half shells are shaped into beads and threaded on a string, the ends of which are fastened to a whale's tooth. This item was so highly valued that it could be used as compensation for murder.

❻ Maori Storehouse (New Zealand, Polynesia)
With elaborately carved outer walls, this was used to store food, farm tools, and weapons.

❼ Shark's Tooth Weapons (*above*: Satawal Island, Micronesia; *below*: Hawaiian Islands, Polynesia [replica])
Owing to the lack of metal technology in Oceania, the sharp teeth of sharks were often used for such weapons as daggers and knuckle-dusters.

❽ War Club (Marquesas Islands, Polynesia)
A human face is carved on the end of the club, and the eyes and nose are all miniature carvings of faces.

❾ Greenstone Club (New Zealand, Polynesia)
Owned only by people of high social status, this was used both as a weapon and as a symbol of authority when speaking in public.

❿ War Club (Samoa Islands, Polynesia)
Teeth are carved on both sides of this club. Battles in Polynesia were fought at close quarters, so a large variety of war clubs are found there.

⓫ Shields
Throughout New Guinea, a shield is an essential element of a warrior's battle gear. Some designs are of guardian spirits invoked for victory in battle, and others are simply intended to frighten the enemy. Ritual was an important element of battle.

⓫ OS 0525, etc.

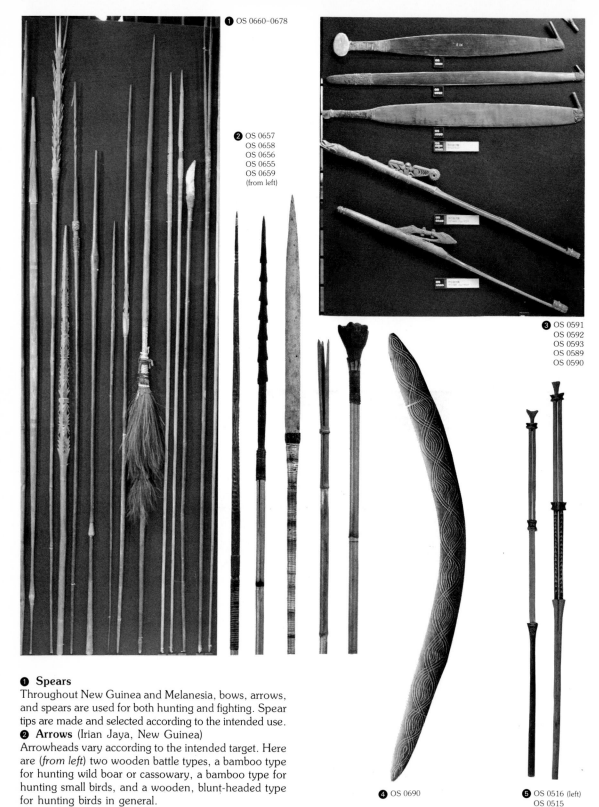

❶ OS 0660–0678

❷ OS 0657
OS 0658
OS 0656
OS 0655
OS 0659
(from left)

❸ OS 0591
OS 0592
OS 0593
OS 0589
OS 0590

❹ OS 0690

❺ OS 0516 (left)
OS 0515

❶ Spears
Throughout New Guinea and Melanesia, bows, arrows, and spears are used for both hunting and fighting. Spear tips are made and selected according to the intended use.

❷ Arrows (Irian Jaya, New Guinea)
Arrowheads vary according to the intended target. Here are (*from left*) two wooden battle types, a bamboo type for hunting wild boar or cassowary, a bamboo type for hunting small birds, and a wooden, blunt-headed type for hunting birds in general.

❸ Spear Throwers (*top three*: Australia; *bottom two*: Madang Province, New Guinea)
Spears travel much farther when they are fitted into the notch and thrown.

❹ Boomerang (Australia)
Curved boomerangs, used for hunting kangaroo, emu, and smaller animals, return to the hand of the thrower. This is engraved with a wave pattern.

❺ Courtship Staffs (Truk Islands, Micronesia)
A young man may declare his love for a girl by putting his courtship staff in her room at night while she is asleep. The girl can identify the man by the engraving on the staff, and may join him outside if she wishes.

❻ OS 0483

❾ OS 0503

⓬ OS 0496

❿ OS 0489

⓫ OS 0508

❽ OS 0075

❼ OS 0501

❻ **Dancing Paddle** (Pohnpei Island, Micronesia)
Characteristically decorated with lattice and chevron patterns, such paddles are brandished and clashed together by dancers.

❼ **Drum** (Solomon Islands, Melanesia)
Used to accompany dances. The body of the drum is carved and painted, and lizard skin is stretched over one end to form the head.

❽ **Slit Gong** (New Hebrides Islands, Melanesia)
This slit gong, made by hollowing out the trunk of a breadfruit tree, is called a *tam-tam* on Ambrym Island.

❾ **Slit Gong** (East Sepik Province, New Guinea)
Called a *garamut*, this slit gong is used both to accompany dances and for communication. It may be beaten, or the drumsticks may be inserted into the slit and drawn back and forth.

❿ **Panpipe** (Simbu Province, New Guinea)
Made by tying together a row of bamboo of different lengths. The order of the pipes varies by region.

⓫ **Pigeon Whistle** (Simbu Province, New Guinea)
Made of clay and used by young men of the Sinasina area to serenade young women in courtship rituals.

⓬ **Bamboo Flute** (East Sepik Province, New Guinea)
A sacred ritual instrument that is only played with other instruments. Its sound is said to represent the voices of spirits.

OS 0853, etc.

② OS 0743

③ OS 0731

The World of Ritual

The religious beliefs of Oceania include polytheism, mythical heroes of particular descent groups, gods of creation, ancestral and other spirits of the dead, and the supernatural power known as *mana*. A people's religious view of the world is manifest in their rituals: Polynesian societies have distinct classes of religious intermediaries, while in Melanesia, New Guinea, and Australia, village religious leaders or hereditary chiefs play important ritual roles. In Polynesia, religious rites were held at stone altars and shrines, while in New Guinea and Melanesia they centered around men's houses and were organized by secret societies. Bodily adornment (including mutilation), cannibalism (in parts of Polynesia), the sacrifice of pigs, and various

24

④ OS 0802

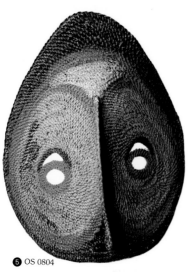

⑤ OS 0804

⑥ OS 0791

dietary, sexual, and verbal taboos were practiced to achieve communion with the gods or other supernatural beings, or to obtain spiritual power. Many activities of daily life were associated with rituals, including yam harvesting, fishing, ocean voyages, rites of passage, house and canoe construction, victory in war, and the investiture of new tribal leaders. Many of the masks and sacred images used in rituals and ancestor worship have great value as folk art.

❶ **Hooks** (East Sepik Province, New Guinea)
Faces representing ancestors are carved on these hooks that are hung on the walls of the men's house. Offerings used in rituals were put in bags and hung on the hooks. Food was also stored this way.

❷ **Ancestral Figure** (New Ireland Island, Melanesia)

A pole carved with human faces, fowls, and wild boar motifs used in ancestor worship rituals.

❸ **Ancestral Figure** (East Sepik Province, New Guinea)
Before this 3.9-meter-tall image of an ancestral spirit, flute music was played to comfort the spirit.

❹ **Mask** (New Britain Island, Melanesia)
Made of *tapa* cloth sewn on a wooden frame, with enormous round eyes and a large mouth with protruding lips. Before donning the mask, dancers would blacken their bodies with charcoal.

❺ **Mask** (East Sepik Province, New Guinea)
This rattan mask is put on a giant yam, and is thus charged with appealing to ancestral spirits for a bountiful harvest.

❻ **Mask** (East Sepik Province, New Guinea)
When this rattan costume is put on, the wearer appears as a manifestation of an ancestor and acts as a mediator between the real world and the spirit world.

① OS 0770

③ OS 0776

④ OS 0821

⑤ OS 0807

② OS 0849

⑥ OS 0841

⑦ OS 0803

① **Crocodile Carving** (East Sepik Province, New Guinea)
This enormous carving decorated the outside of the men's house at the level of the raised floor, and the village's guardian deity was believed to reside in it.

② **Hook** (East Sepik Province, New Guinea)
The upper part of this hook has a carving of a human face, with inlaid cowries for eyes. In rituals, offerings to ancestral spirits are hung on the hooks.

③ **Mask** (East Sepik Province, New Guinea)
Decorated with bird feathers, shells, and boar tusks, with a long, beak-like nose.

④ **Mask** (East Sepik Province, New Guinea)
Shells are embedded in clay on a tortoiseshell base in this mask of the Iatmul people.

⑤ **Mask** (East Sepik Province, New Guinea)
A carving of an ancestor's face, ornamented with boar tusks, cassowary feathers, and shells.

⑥ **Mask** (Mortlock Islands, Micronesia)
Representing a man's face with an ornamental comb, this is hung on a post of a house or men's house and worshiped as the guardian deity of war.

⑦ **Mask** (New Ireland Island, Melanesia)
A Malagan-style mask. The hair is styled in an ancient fashion, but some hair has been cut off at the temples.

⑧ **Ceremonial Chair** (East Sepik Province, New Guinea)
In rites, a ritual orator places leaves and branches of a special tree on the ceremonial chair and then stands beside it to relay the words of the ancestral spirit.

❶ OS 0763

❽ OS 0769

❾ OS 0859

❿ OS 0738

⓬ OS 0764

❾ Temple Guardian Figure (replica) (Hawaiian Islands, Polynesia)
This god of war was placed inside a temple platform. The pose is short, thrusting, and aggressive, and the figure has a characteristic mouth in the shape of a figure of eight.

❿ Ancestral Image (Ulithi Islands, Micronesia)
Worshiped as an image or sent out to sea in memorial services for the spirits of the dead. The design painted on the body represents a tattoo, a traditional form of adornment.

⓫ Cult Figure (East Sepik Province, New Guinea)
The god of war and hunting, guardian deity of adult men, reputedly forbidden to be seen by women and children.

⓬ Wind Charm (Satawal Island, Micronesia)
A guardian deity of navigation, providing protection on long voyages and only possessed by skilled navigators.

27

❶ OS 0923

❷ OS 0919

❶ **Sand Painting** (Central Desert, N.T., Australia)
Contemporary sand painting is usually done by men with acrylic paints on canvas. This depicts a central desert creation myth.

❷ **Bark Painting** (Arnhem Land, N.T., Australia)
A picture of totems and spirit myths, drawn on eucalyptus bark with natural pigment.

❸ **Batik, Grave Markers, and Ancestral Figures** (Central Desert, N.T., Australia)
In the background is a traditional abstract pattern used by Pitjantjara women, reproduced here with modern batik methods.

❹ **Grave Marker** (Arnhem Land, N.T., Australia)
Pukamani poles of the Tiwi people are placed around a grave to prevent the soul of the dead person from wandering.

❸ OS 0922 · 0926 · 0928 · 0929–0937   ❹ OS 0927

Australian Aborigines

The popular image of Australian Aborigines is of a people that uses the boomerang, but, in fact, it is not very effective as a weapon and was only used by a small segment of the population, which shows the extent of our misconceptions. According to the evidence of archaeological excavations, the ancestors of the Australian Aborigines migrated about 50,000 years ago from Southeast Asia, moving from island to island until they reached the Australian coastal forests and finally ventured into the arid interior. In the course of migrating and adapting to a variety of natural environments, about 600 tribes, or linguistic groups, were formed. In the eighteenth century, just prior to the first contact with Europeans, the Aborigines were estimated to number around 300,000. They were hunters and gatherers, who, in small bands of twenty to thirty, routinely traveled great distances in search of food. Nomadic life meant that material possessions were limited to just a few items such as spears, spearthrowers, digging sticks, and net bags, but the Aborigines possessed a rich spiritual culture of songs, dances, myths, legends, traditions, and various arts. Modern Aboriginal bark painting, carving, batik, and acrylic painting vividly convey their spiritual world.

The Cultures of the Americas

Tens of thousands of years ago in North and South America, distinct cultures had already developed, the most outstanding being the Aztec, Maya, and Inca civilizations with their distinct social structures, religions, and arts. Even nowadays, whether in the Arctic, the northwest coastal region, the Andes, or the Amazonian basin, the lifestyles reveal features that are especially adapted to the environment.

Over 20,000 years ago, a group of people crossed the region of the Bering Strait to reach the New World. These, the first "Americans," were Northeast Asians of the Upper Paleolithic period who were following the movements of the animals they hunted. Their migration from what is now Siberia occurred in waves, with the earliest emigrants to North America gradually moving south down the ice-free corridor east of the Rocky Mountains, and the last ones being the Eskimo, or Inuit. Remains have been found the length of both North and South America dating from 10,000 years ago, so we know that even at that time there were people living at the southern tip of South America.

By 5000 B.C., agriculture had begun in scattered areas, and simultaneously local cultures made their appearance. By 2000 B.C., a settled lifestyle revolving around the cultivation of such plants as maize, squash, chili, and beans existed in Mexico and the Central Andes, and by 1000 B.C. civilized societies had developed, such as those of the predecessors of the Aztecs, Mayas, and Incas. Thus, after Columbus "discovered" America, the Spanish "conquerors" were astonished to encounter societies with a high degree of organization.

Hunters and gatherers lived in the Arctic, in the subarctic forests, on the Northwest Coast, and on the Great Plains of North America, and in South America on the Pampas and in Patagonia. The Arctic Eskimo, or Inuit, made the maximum use of the limited resources to adapt to a harsh environment. On the Northwest Coast, people took advantage of the resources of forests, rivers, and the ocean to organize societies with large populations centered around chiefs.

In such areas as the southwestern and eastern regions of North America, maize was the primary crop, and it was cultivated with small-scale irrigation and slash-and-burn systems. People in the southern Andes cultivated maize and potatoes, and raised llamas and alpacas. In the Caribbean region, chiefdoms of various sizes existed, each with its own complex labor and social stratifications. And in the vast river basins of the Amazon and the Orinoco, slash-and-burn agriculture, hunting, and fishing supported settled village life.

After such distinctive cultures evolved, the Americas were rapidly "conquered" and colonized following their discovery by Columbus. Many civilizations and societies disappeared amid this drastic historical upheaval. But even today, nearly five hundred years later, the cultures of the Americas retain something of their traditions and potential. In the tropical forests of the Amazon and the Orinoco, some 400,000 people still live in small, isolated communities. Under colonial rule, the huge populations of Mesoamerica and the Andean highlands saw a marked decline, but the cultural traditions of the survivors were integrated with European elements, resulting in the present-day peasant culture.

The exhibit presents cultural features of the indigenous inhabitants of the Americas, which were adapted to the great variety of natural environments. Beginning with a display of the legacy of ancient American civilizations, it shows daily life and festivals in five cultural areas: the Arctic, the Pacific Northwest Coast, Mesoamerica, the Central Andes, and the Amazon. (Hiroyasu Tomoeda)

View of a village in southwest Alaska.

Mixe women at market selling tepache liquor.

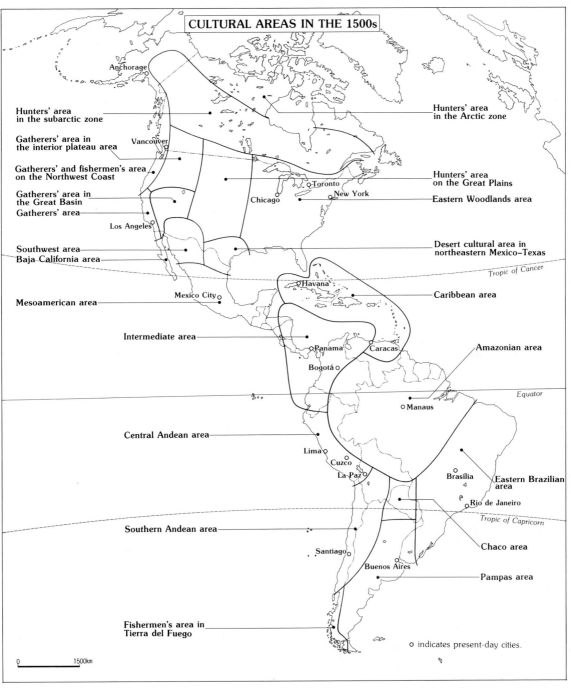

CULTURAL AREAS IN THE 1500s

Anchorage

Hunters' area
in the subarctic zone

Gatherers' area in
the interior plateau area

Vancouver

Gatherers' and fishermen's area
on the Northwest Coast

Gatherers' area in
the Great Basin

Gatherers' area

Los Angeles

Southwest area

Baja California area

Mesoamerican area

Mexico City

Intermediate area

Panama

Bogotá

Central Andean area

Lima

Cuzco

La Paz

Southern Andean area

Santiago

Fishermen's area in
Tierra del Fuego

Hunters' area
in the Arctic zone

Toronto

Chicago

New York

Hunters' area
on the Great Plains

Eastern Woodlands area

Desert cultural area in
northeastern Mexico–Texas

Tropic of Cancer

Havana

Caribbean area

Caracas

Amazonian area

Equator

Manaus

Brasília

Eastern Brazilian
area

Rio de Janeiro

Tropic of Capricorn

Chaco area

Buenos Aires

Pampas area

o indicates present-day cities.

0   1500km

Llamas in the high Andes.

A house on stilts in the Amazonian area.

Ancient American Civilizations

The term "Ancient America" refers to the time before the arrival of Columbus in 1492 and subsequent contact with other Europeans who crossed the Atlantic, and it is also known as the pre-Columbian or pre-Spanish era. Only two regions developed to the stage that might be regarded as ancient civilizations: Mesoamerica, represented by the Aztec and Mayan civilizations, and the Central Andes, with the civilization of the Incas. These civilizations were based on the intensive cultivation of corn that began around 1500 B.C. With the exception of the Aztecs, the Mayans, the Zapotecs, and a few other Mesoamerican cultures, these societies possessed neither a written script nor iron, and thus their development stopped at the level of the New Stone Age. However, their large populations were well organized politically and socially, and they erected huge religious structures, engaged in engineering projects, and produced superb crafts. In these fields, they were in no way inferior to the civilizations of the Old World. From the sixteenth century, the ancient civilizations of the Americas were conquered and destroyed by the Spaniards, but many of their traditional spiritual and technical aspects survive today in the cultures of the indigenous peoples.

❶ **Aztec Calendar Stone** (replica) (The Aztecs, Mexico)
The original of this typical carving of ancient American culture is in the National Museum of Anthropology, Mexico City.
❷ **Mayan Relief Carving** (replica) (The Mayas, Mexico)
A decoration from the back wall of a palace, with Mayan pictorial script carved on both sides of a central ritual scene.
❸–❺ **Clay Vessels** (replicas) (Peru)
Of all clay vessels of the ancient American civilizations, those from the Central Andes region display the richest variety in sculptural form, color, and design.

❶ AM 0026

❷ AM 0027

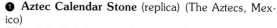

❸ AM 0005

❹ AM 0007

❺ AM 0006

North America

The environments of North America range from the tundra region of the Arctic to the deserts of the southwest, and the cultures of the indigenous peoples—the Eskimo and the Indians—developed in various ways as they adapted to their environment. In the Arctic, the Eskimo, or Inuit, settled across the entire continent, from the Bering Strait in the west to Greenland in the east. Although their main activities were hunting for marine animals on the ice or for caribou in the interior, and fishing in the oceans and rivers, there were considerable regional differences. The Eskimo's basic social unit consisted of several families, and larger villages did not develop. Characteristic of the Eskimo were their careful use of limited resources and their techniques for coping with the cold. The Pacific northwest coastal region extends from southeastern Alaska to northern California, which is warmed by the Kuroshio, or Japan Current, and is rich in fish and shellfish, marine and land animals, and forests. There, large stable villages and stratified societies developed, sustained by a regular source of food from the ocean, and fine artistry in wood and other natural materials was evident there.

6 Winter Outer Clothing (The Eskimo, Alaska)
Made of caribou hide, this is ideal for bitterly cold regions as it is designed to trap several layers of air around the body.

7 Women's Overshoes (The Inuit, Greenland)
Made of well-tanned caribou hide, with decoration along the seams.

8 Snow Goggles (The Inuit, Greenland)
Made from driftwood and caribou-hide cord, these cut down the amount of light reflected into the eyes off snow and ice.

9 Dog Sled (The Inuit, Canada)
A thin strip of wood is attached to the runners, and notches are cut into the crosspieces so they can be lashed in place with leather cord.

10–11 Leather Bags (The Inuit, Greenland)
Made of tanned caribou hide, these are used to carry light items such as wild strawberries or smoked fish.

12 Snowshoes (The Eskimo, Alaska)
The elongated wooden frames have webbing of cord made of caribou sinews or hide.

13 Kayak (The Inuit, Canada)
Tanned caribou hide is stretched over a wooden frame in such a canoe, which is propelled by a wooden paddle.

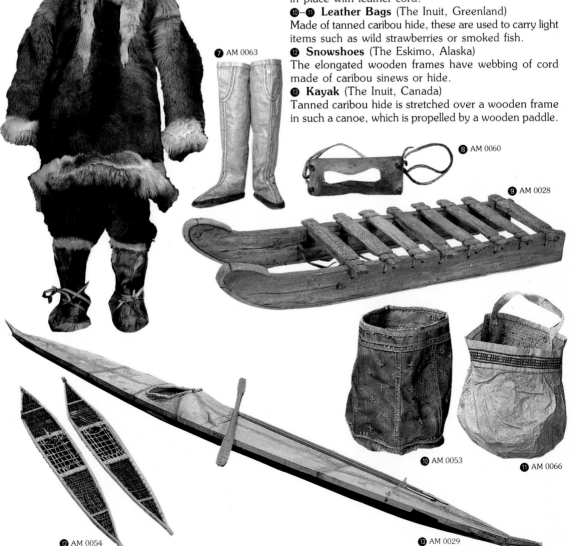

6 AM 0160
AM 0161
AM 0414

7 AM 0063

8 AM 0060

9 AM 0028

10 AM 0053

11 AM 0066

12 AM 0054

13 AM 0029

③ AM 0459

④ AM 0108

① AM 0456

①–④ Masks (The Eskimo and Inuit, Alaska and Greenland)

Made from driftwood and caribou hide, these are used for ritual dancing. Most masks from southwestern Alaska have attached circular decorations, while those from Greenland have tattoos and feather beards.

⑤ Drum and Stick (The Eskimo, Alaska)

Tanned caribou hide is stretched over a round wooden frame with a handle, and the drum is beaten with a thin branch at ritual dances.

⑥ Magical Amulets (The Inuit, Greenland)

These walrus tooth carvings demonstrate excellent technique. To place a curse on someone, a figure like one of these *tupilak* is buried outside that person's house.

⑤ AM 0058
AM 0056

② AM 0458

⑥ AM 0461–0465

7 Wooden Club for Killing Fish (The Kwakiutl, British Columbia)
Used to kill newly caught salmon, such clubs are found throughout the North Pacific region.

8 Fish Hook (The Nootka, British Columbia)
Especially for halibut, this has a figure of the owner carved on the upper wooden portion.

9–11 Spoons (The Tlingit, Southeastern Alaska)
Made of wood or mountain goat horn.

12 Ladle (British Columbia)
Shell decoration has been inlaid in the handle.

13 Wooden Bowl (The Kwakiutl, British Columbia)

14–15 Cooking Fat Containers (The Kwakiutl, British Columbia)
Fat taken from a variety of smelt is an essential seasoning.

16 Pipe (The Tlingit, Southeast Alaska)
Smoke was believed to be purifying, so such pipes were essential ritual implements.

17 Copper Crest (The Nishka, British Columbia)
Each crest tells the genealogy of its owner. Such crests were used in rituals and were once considered symbols of wealth.

④ AM 0517

⑤ AM 0520

⑥ AM 0524

⑦ AM 0514

① AM 0509

② AM 0510

③ AM 0505

①–② Clothing (The Quiché, Guatemala)
Everyday wear for men and women of Chichicastenango. Few villages now preserve traditional dress for both men and women.

③ Huipil, or Woman's Overblouse (The Cakchiquel, Guatemala)
Everyday wear in San Pedro Sacatepéquez.

④–⑤ Vessels (The Mixe, Oaxaca, Mexico; ④ from Mixistlán; ⑤ from Tamazulapam)
Together with Tlahuitoltepec, these villages make earthenware vessels to sell to other villages. ⑤ is shoe-shaped so it can easily be inserted among firewood.

⑥ Bowl (The Mixtec, Oaxaca, Mexico)
Many varieties of such simple bowls are found on the Mixtec plateau and in coastal areas.

⑦ Water Pot (The Tlapanec, Guerrero, Mexico)
Made in the village of Zacualpán, with handles through which a rope was threaded.

Mesoamerica

The term "Mesoamerica" refers to the cultural region comprising Mexico, Guatemala, and El Salvador, as well as some parts of Honduras, Nicaragua, and Costa Rica. Many indigenous peoples still live in this region, with cultures and societies that combine indigenous and colonial elements. Their barely subsistence standard of living depends on maize, frijol beans, and squash, supplemented by seasonal work on plantations and large farms. Material culture in the villages is simple, but beautiful, colorful pottery is produced, and superbly patterned textiles are woven with backstrap looms. Festivals are marked by fireworks and music, with masked dances and dramas. On the day before Easter Sunday, Judas dolls are burned, and on All Souls' Day skeleton dolls and candy are sold.

8 AM 0472

9 AM 0476

10 AM 0469

11 AM 0468

12 AM 0493

13 AM 0494

14 AM 0503

15 AM 0504

16 AM 0483

17 AM 0481

8–**11** **"Tiger" Masks** (Mexico)

"Tiger" refers to jaguars, which are symbolic of the power of nature. A dancer wearing a "tiger" mask figures in dance-dramas such as *tecuani*, *tigre*, and *tlacololero*. After destroying crops and troubling farm animals and people, the tiger is shot and leaves the stage. Such masks are found throughout Mesoamerica, although these from the state of Guerrero are distinctive both in technique and in design.

12–**13** **Devil Masks** (Mexico)

Spirit masks modeled on animals and other creatures existed before the arrival of the Spaniards, but the mission-aries are said to have put horns on the masks to represent the Devil. Such masks are used at carnivals and in dance-dramas showing the supremacy of Catholicism.

14–**15** **Judas Dolls** (Mexico)

Symbols of evil, these are burned the day before Easter Sunday. In rural areas, they are usually made by stuffing old clothes with straw.

16–**17** **Carnival Masks** (Mexico)

Especially numerous in the Mexican states of Puebla, Veracruz, and Morelos. **16** is a Chinelo mask from Morelos; **17** is from Veracruz.

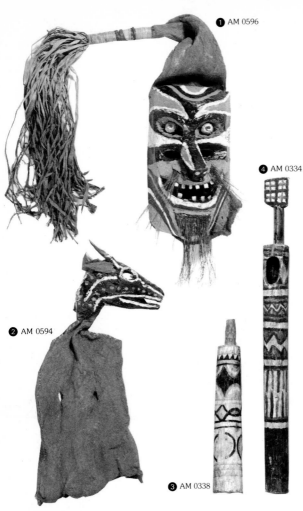

① AM 0596

② AM 0594

③ AM 0338

④ AM 0334

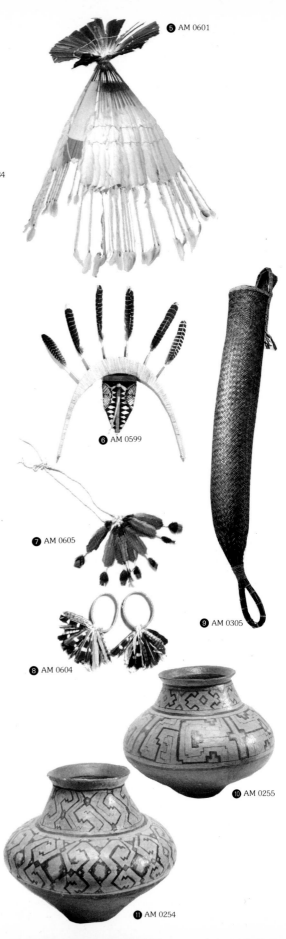

⑤ AM 0601

⑥ AM 0599

⑦ AM 0605

⑧ AM 0604

⑨ AM 0305

⑩ AM 0255

⑪ AM 0254

South America

The South American continent has several very different climatic regions: the Andes mountain range along the Pacific coast, tropical rain forests and plains (called the Pampas) to the east of the Andes, and Patagonia at the southern tip. The lives of people in the Central Andean highlands represent a mixture of traditions from Incan times and foreign elements introduced after contact with Europeans. For example, most festivals combine European-style costumes and masks with traditional flutes and drums. Despite the introduction of modern clothing, domesticated animals such as cattle and sheep, and crops such as barley, weaving and pottery-making and other daily activities still employ techniques that have hardly changed before the arrival of the Europeans. In the tropical lowlands, some tribes have died out or have been forced to change drastically through contact with Europeans and recent rapid development. Daily life in these regions depends on slash-and-burn cultivation of manioc, plantain, and sweet potatoes, as well as on hunting peccary, tapir, and other animals. For dances in harvest and hunting rituals, rites of passage, and other ceremonies, participants decorate their heads and arms with feathers and don masks representing mythical beings and animals.

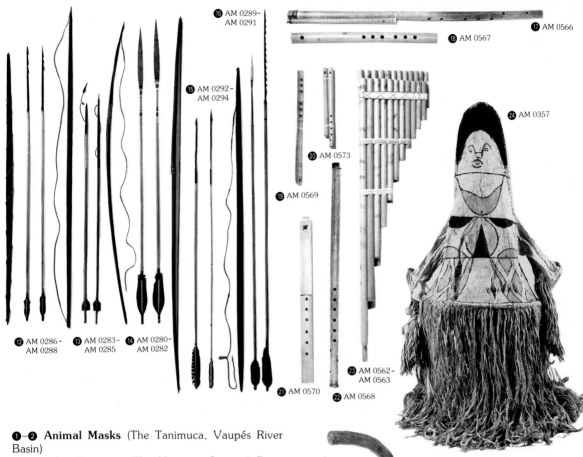

⑯ AM 0289-AM 0291

⑰ AM 0566

⑱ AM 0567

⑮ AM 0292-AM 0294

⑳ AM 0573

⑲ AM 0569

② AM 0357

⑫ AM 0286-AM 0288   ⑬ AM 0283-AM 0285   ⑭ AM 0280-AM 0282

㉓ AM 0562-AM 0563

㉑ AM 0570

㉒ AM 0568

❶–❷ **Animal Masks** (The Tanimuca, Vaupés River Basin)

❸ **Wooden Trumpet** (The Yucuna, Caquetá River Basin)

❹ **Dancing Stave** (The Tukano, Vaupés River Basin) Found throughout the northwestern Amazon basin, this hollow instrument is beaten on the ground to set the rhythm for dances.

❺ **Head Ornament** (The Carajá, Mato Grosso)

❻ **Mask** (The Kuikuru, Mato Grosso)

❼ **Necklace** (The Cayapó, Mato Grosso)

❽ **Bracelets** (The Cayapó, Mato Grosso)

❾ **Manioc Squeezer** (The Ye'cuana, Guiana Highlands)
This is packed with grated manioc (also called cassava) and squeezed by being pulled taut with a lever to eliminate the poison in the tuber and excess liquid.

❿–⓫ **Pots** (The Piro, Urubamba River Basin)
Earthenware vessels made by women of the Piro tribe are an expression of the bond between mother and daughter or between sisters. A pot is exchanged at wedding ceremonies for a man's bow and arrows.

⓬–⓰ **Bows and Arrows** (⓬ The Campa, Lower Apurímac River Basin; ⓭ The Miranya, Caquetá River Basin; ⓮ The Amahuaca, Upper Purús River Basin; ⓯ The Camayura, Mato Grosso; ⓰ The Machiguenga, Upper Madre de Dios River Basin)

⓱–㉓ **Flutes** (⓳ Potosí, Bolivia; *the others*: Huarata Grande, Bolivia)
Many types of flutes are used in the highlands of Bolivia, some of wood, others of a bamboo-like plant called *caña.* The general name for flutes is *viento,* meaning "wind," but each type also has a name: *flauta, moseño, sampoña, pinquillo, tarca,* or *quena.* The instrument or combination of instruments to be used at each festival and ritual is fixed.

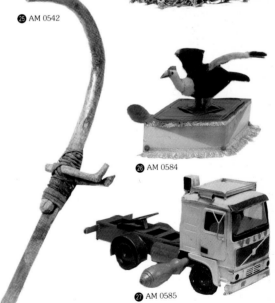

㉕ AM 0542

㉖ AM 0584

㉗ AM 0585

㉔ **Mask** (The Tucano, Vaupés River Basin)
Masks made of tree bark and palm fronds are found throughout the tropical lowlands of South America and used in such rituals as coming-of-age ceremonies, fertility rites, and rites for the dead.

㉕ **Foot Plow** (La Paz, Bolivia)
Used in the Central Andes since before the arrival of the Spanish, mainly for planting potatoes on sloping land.

㉖–㉗ **Rattles** (La Paz, Bolivia)
Used in the popular Morenada dance in the highlands of Bolivia. Shapes vary by village and city district.

② AM 0539

③ AM 0546

④ AM 0557

⑥ AM 0530

① AM 0540

⑤ AM 0536

❶–❷ Clothing (Amarete, Bolivia)
Clothing from northwest Bolivia near the Peruvian border. The woman's woven wool dress, called an *acus*, and the head-covering worn under the woman's hat probably predate the arrival of the Spaniards.

❸–❹ Masks (❸ La Paz, Bolivia; ❹ Saquisilí, Ecuador)
❸ is used in the typical Diablada dance in the southern Andes. Some masks are made of tin, others of plaster.

❺ Wrapping Cloth (Cuzco, Peru)
Used mainly by women for carrying money, coca leaves, or food.

❻ Coca Bag (Tarabuco, Bolivia)
Chewing coca leaves is a widespread habit. The size, design, and decoration of bags differ by region, and they are carried only by men and hold the coca leaves that are also indispensable for rituals.

❼ Shawl (Charazani, Bolivia)
Women also use this as a wrapping cloth, a ground cloth, or a tablecloth.

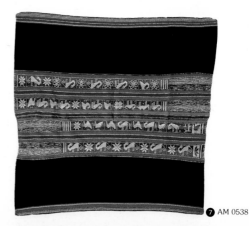

❼ AM 0538

The Cultures of Europe

Europe occupies only a small portion of the Eurasian continent, but it has seen the emergence of numerous cultures and complex ethnic groups. Animal husbandry and farming form the basis of all European ways of life, which are characterized by the prevalence of milk and grains and, in some regions, the cultivation of grapes. The plurality of local cultures is evident in the wooden houses of the north and the stone houses of the south, and in the richness and variety of European clothing and articles of daily life.

The French poet Paul Valéry once suggested that Europe is nothing but a peninsula on the vast continent of Eurasia. Its mountains, plains, and seas are intricately linked, and the warm currents and prevailing westerly winds of the Atlantic bring an oceanic influence to northwestern Europe, making areas even in the far north habitable, while the Mediterranean region south of the Alps is warm and dry. From antiquity, groups of people have constantly moved back and forth across this narrow stage that is Europe and created a mosaic-like diversity of cultures.

The region north of the Alps was covered with forests until the Middle Ages, when the land was put under cultivation and converted into pastures and fields. Before then, agriculture and animal husbandry seemed to consist of slash-and-burn cultivation. In the three-field system of agriculture believed to have been introduced in the Middle Ages, the cultivation of fields and the raising of livestock were coordinated, and from about the eighteenth century many forms of crop rotation were adopted, making land use more efficient. Thus, the occupation that has supported the basic cultures of Europe is clearly grain cultivation combined with the raising of domesticated animals. In the Mediterranean region and the areas stretching from central France to the middle reaches of the Rhine, the cultivation of grapes for wine-making is important.

The primary aim of the exhibit is to show the types of work that formed the basis of European life. Thus, it focuses on mixed farming, represented by milk and grain production, and on grape cultivation.

Christianity was the common spiritual support for the whole of Europe, but behind it lay the indigenous basic cultures. For example, in German farming villages, the Christian celebration of Easter falls near the beginning of spring, Pentecost is celebrated fifty days after Easter, and St. John's Day falls on the summer solstice. These Christian events coincide with the Germanic calendar of events established in accordance with the seasonal rhythm of agriculture. The custom of erecting a maypole or a birch or beech tree in a doorway or outdoors, fire festivals, and mask and costume parades all predate Christianity and survive in various places throughout Europe. Christianity became established in European society as it absorbed this fundamental culture.

In the Mediterranean region, stone was widely used as a material in daily life, including for the construction of houses. North of the Alps are splendid houses built of logs, and in northern Europe houses are made of wood, as are many articles of daily life. Superb pieces of furniture and household utensils have been handed down over the generations, and each is steeped in the rich, regional wisdom of daily life. This blend of traditional ethnic culture and rich basic culture is reflected in the way clothing and various articles are used in different regions. The second part of the exhibit emphasizes the traditional cultures of the common people of Europe, whose daily lives centered around clothing, foods, and dwellings passed down from their ancestors.

Today, most of Europe is occupied by groups of people who use one of the Indo-European languages. The Latin peoples extend west from the northern shores of the Mediterranean to the Rhine, the Germanic peoples occupy the area north of the line formed by the Alps and the Rhine, and the Slavic peoples live in the remaining eastern part of Europe. Scattered among these three great European peoples are smaller groups, some of whom do not speak Indo-European languages.

A display of the distinct culture of the Gypsies has been included in the European exhibit as an example of a small ethnic group living on the Continent. (Hisatsugu Sugimoto, Yuiti Wada)

Harvesting in France (late 19th century).

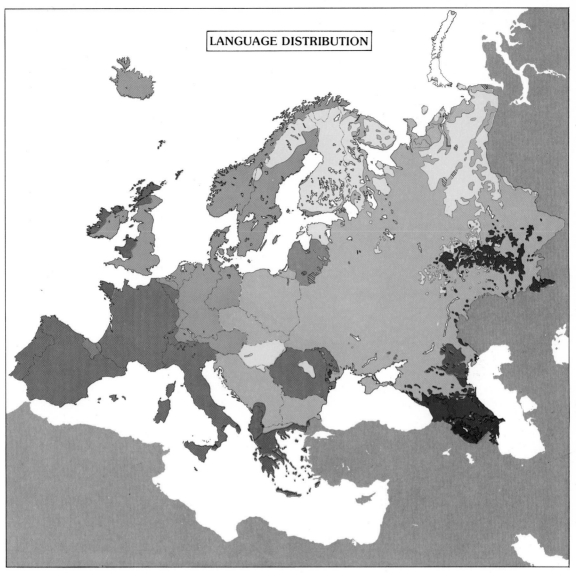

LANGUAGE DISTRIBUTION

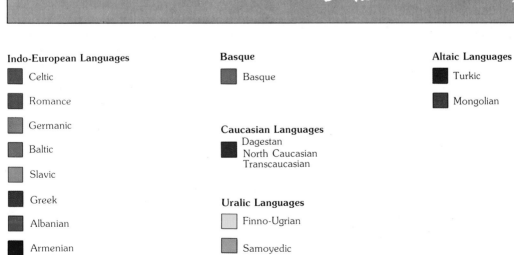

Indo-European Languages

- Celtic
- Romance
- Germanic
- Baltic
- Slavic
- Greek
- Albanian
- Armenian
- Iranian

Basque

- Basque

Caucasian Languages

- Dagestan
  North Caucasian
  Transcaucasian

Uralic Languages

- Finno-Ugrian
- Samoyedic

Altaic Languages

- Turkic
- Mongolian

① YO 0026

② YO 0027

③ YO 0028

④ YO 0085・0087

⑤ YO 0029

⑥ YO 0030

Diversified Farming and Food Processing

Farming combining the cultivation of grains and the raising of domesticated animals was the traditional form of livelihood in Europe. The land north of the Alps was once covered with forests, but these were gradually cleared for cultivation. The three-field system of agriculture, which brought together upland farming and animal husbandry, developed in the period from the Middle Ages up to the modern era. In the latter half of the nineteenth century, when wheat flour was imported from North America, feed grains were cultivated by crop rotation methods, and farming centered on raising domesticated animals. Dairy farming for milk, butter, and cheese developed especially along the northern coasts and the Baltic Sea, as well as in Switzerland. In the Mediterranean regions, with hot, dry summers and wet winters, drought-resistant fruit trees such as olives, lemons, figs, and grapevines were widely cultivated, and the wine made from the grapes permeated lifestyles there. The exhibit assembles objects related to the production of grain, milk, and grapes, and on the walls are reproductions of etchings of crop and dairy farming and wine-making.

1 Butter Churn and Stirrer (Helsinki, Southern Finland)
While the churn is held still by gripping the handle, the round end of the stirrer is moved up and down in the churn.

2 Butter Churn (Berry Region, Central France)
When the handle is turned, an interior wheel made of boards revolves at speed.

3 Butter Cask (Vihti, Southern Finland)
Of juniper wood and dating to the late nineteenth century. The art of cask-making existed in Finland from the early fourth century.

4 Butter Jars (Berry Region, Central France)
Earthenware containers with distinctive handles.

5 Butter Mold (Berry Region, Central France)

6 Cheese Mold (Mäntsälä, Southern Finland)
Curdled milk is put into the mold after excess liquid has been drained off.

7 Grape Press (Berry Region, Central France)
Used to extract grape juice, which is then fermented; now replaced by machines.

8 Drinking Vessel (Lammi, Southern Finland)
Made of fragrant wood of trees of the pine family, such as juniper, these vessels were for *sahti*, a local brew.

9 Wine Cask Spigot (Berry Region, Central France)

10 Wine Pitcher (Berry Region, Central France)

11 Horse Yoke (Finland)
This yoke has little carving other than the bird motifs, but in some regions yokes are covered with carving.

7 YO 0053

9 YO 0060

8 YO 0081

10 YO 0058

11 YO 0016

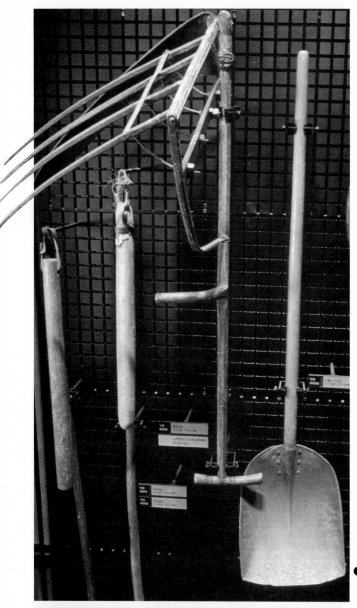

❸ YO 0031

❹ YO 0004
YO 0003

❶ YO 0011
YO 0012
YO 0010
YO 0006

❺ YO 0005

❷ YO 0007

❶ Farming Tools (Berry Region, Central France)
These are (*from left*) flails, a rake-sickle, and a wheat shovel. The end of the long handle of the rake-sickle is held in the left hand, and the short handle in the right hand.
❷ Plow (Lohja, Southern Finland)
❸ Pitchfork (Berry Region, Central France)

❹ Wheat Bag and Stand (Berry Region, Central France)
The side of the bag bears the merchant's name and that of his village.
❺ Wheat Measure (Berry Region, Central France)
Consisting of a funnel and a measure, with an attached roller for leveling the wheat being measured.

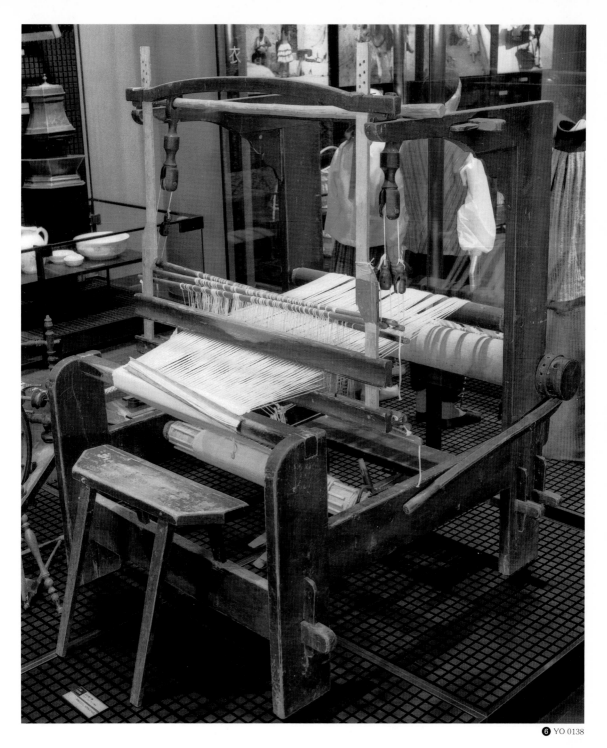

Daily Life

The food of Europe consisted fundamentally of bread and dairy products, with meat coming to occupy a major place in ordinary people's diet only relatively recently. Another characteristic of food was the development of techniques to preserve perishables. The materials of European dwellings are wood and stone, with log houses in northern Europe, which is rich in lumber, and other wooden houses in the mountainous areas of eastern Europe and the Alps. In the Mediterranean region, dwellings have stone walls covered with white plaster. Among articles on display showing daily life in Europe are ethnic clothing, furniture, carpets, and looms. Unlike Japanese clothing, which gives the impression of being a flat piece of fabric, European clothes are basically cylindrical in shape, as seen in skirts and trousers. On the walls of the display area are illustrations of room interiors and of representative houses from different regions.

❻ **Loom** (Lohja, Southern Finland)

❶ YO 0213

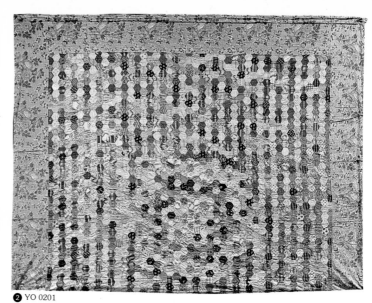

❷ YO 0201

❶ Sampler (London, England)
A young girl's embroidery practice piece with a poem.
❷ Patchwork (London, England)
In the nineteenth century, patchwork like this was used for bedspreads and cushions covers.
❸ Clothes Chest (Spain)
❹ Stages in Making Wooden Clogs (Berry, Central France)
Wooden clogs are thought of as a product of Holland, but they were also found throughout France, where they are still used in farming villages, although now more rarely. Each shoe is made from one block of wood, and occasionally leather is placed over the instep or hobnails are used to strengthen the sole.

❺ Spinning Wheel Distaff (Western Finland)
In Finland, a distaff was usually a small board, and it was customary for a man to carve one to present to his bride.
❻ Ryijy Carpet (Helsinki, Southern Finland)
Traditional carpets have ethnic designs, such as the Tree of Life and folk-tale characters.
❼ Spinning Wheel (Lohja, Southern Finland)
The spinning wheel replaced the spindle in Finland around the sixteenth century. This piece dates to the nineteenth century.
❽–❿ Birch Bark Articles (**❽** Backpack [Tuusniemi, Eastern Finland]; **❾** Shoes [Savo, Eastern Finland]; **❿** Horn [Helsinki, Southern Finland])
Bark is carefully stripped off the trees that proliferate in the region and made into such articles as these.

❸ YO 0131

❹ YO 0132

5 YO 0170

6 YO 0149

7 YO 0137

8 YO 0160

9 YO 0161

10 YO 0159

49

❶ YO 0141
YO 0142

❷ YO 0156

❸ YO 0146

❹ YO 0208

❻ YO 0127

❼ YO 0148

❺ YO 0128

❶ **Sofa-bed** (Helsinki, Southern Finland)
Many northern European sofa-beds have an open-frame back. The bedspread is made of a handwoven fabric called *raanu*, which comes from Lapua in central-western Finland).

❷ **Water Tank and Basin** (Berry, Central France)
This simple device to provide water for washing the hands, called a *fontaine* (fountain) in French, was popular from the seventeenth century on. This piece dates to the eighteenth century.

❸ **Cradle** (Eastern Finland)
Cradles in eastern Finland are usually decorated in shades of red.

❹ **Man's and Woman's Stools from a Pub, or Bar** (London, England)

❺ **Chair** (Helsinki, Southern Finland)

❻ **Table** (Helsinki, Southern Finland)
Made of wood and sturdily constructed, usually without any nails.

❼ **Bed-warmer** (Berry, Central France)
This eighteenth-century one is made of copper.

 YO 0192

The Gypsies

Of the many small ethnic groups in Europe, the Gypsies—an itinerant people renowned for music and fortune-telling who came to Europe at the beginning of the fifteenth century—hold a special place. Although each European country encourages the Gypsies to settle, if we take the example of the 80,000 Gypsies said to be in France, about 20,000 continue to move from place to place. Of these, only 2 percent live in horse-drawn caravans like the one displayed, while the others use trailers and the like. In Finland, a newspaper is published especially for the Gypsies, but most of the articles are written in Finnish, except for about 5 percent which is in the Gypsy language. The number of people who can speak the language, which is based on the vocabulary and structure of the Indo-Aryan language of western India, the land of their forefathers, is decreasing rapidly.

❽ Horse-drawn Gypsy Caravan (Berry, Central France)
On average, a family of five to eight people live in one horse-drawn wagon, called a *roulotte*. Each caravan is painted in certain colors to serve as an address for mail delivery, and Gypsies are not allowed to change these colors without official permission. The carvings of horses' heads flank the door.

❸ YO 0177

❹ YO 0173

❷ YO 0198

❶ **Interior of a Horse-drawn Gypsy Caravan** (Berry, Central France)
The parents sleep in the bed at the back, the daughters underneath it in the area closed off by doors, and the sons spread their bedding on the floor. The stove is in the left foreground.
❷ **Gypsy Doll** (Berry, Central France)
❸–❹ **Hand-made Articles** (Berry, Central France)
Articles such as these baskets of willow are made and sold as the Gypsies move around.

The Cultures of Africa

The vast area lying to the south of the Sahara Desert has fostered many distinctive cultures. Several peoples established kingdoms on the savannas and in the forests there, and they developed grain farming and cattle-herding cultures, as well as the superb plastic arts seen in the sculptures, masks, and objects of daily life.

The African continent comprises 20 percent of the total land in the world, and anthropologically it can be divided into North Africa and Africa south of the Sahara Desert. North Africa—extending north of the Sahara along the Mediterranean Sea and inhabited by Caucasoids such as Arabs and Berbers—saw the flowering of the ancient kingdoms of Egypt and other Mediterranean civilizations. This area is now dominated by Islamic culture, with Arabic spoken widely.

The people who live south of the Sahara Desert are mostly negroid. More than 1,000 ethnic groups, each with its own language and lifestyle, live in this region and form the core of Black African ethnic culture. The Africa exhibit focuses on this region and highlights several themes.

Africa was once called the "dark continent" because the geography and cultures of the interior were unknown to the rest of the world, which led to the mistaken impression that Africa had no civilization or history that was worthy of study. However, research this century has revealed that many kingdoms flourished and developed their own civilizations in Sub-Saharan Africa, and many independent nations today are named after those former kingdoms. Thus, the pejorative phrase "dark continent" is now obsolete.

Most of the peoples living in the tropical rain forest and savanna regions follow agricultural ways of life. In the rain forest, root crops, such as yams and taros, and plantains are cultivated as staple foods, while in the savanna, sorghum, pearl millet, finger millet, and maize are the main crops. Cash crops such as oil palms, cacao, coffee, and cotton are also widely grown.

In the vast savannas stretching from West Africa to East Africa, nomadic peoples engaged in raising cattle are scattered among farming communities. Peoples who lived by hunting and gathering are thought to have once inhabited areas all over Africa, but today the Pygmies in the rain forests of the Congo basin and the San bushmen of the Kalahari Desert are among the few remaining hunters and gatherers.

The peoples of Black Africa have created many distinctive lifestyles, which are reflected in the utensils and ornaments of everyday life, such as calabashes, earthenware vessels, dyed and woven textiles, and brassware. Perhaps the most remarkable art objects are the masks, sculptures, and other objects that embody ancestral spirits and heroes remembered through oral tradition. Black Africa is a treasury of folk crafts, and these have greatly influenced modern Western crafts.

Since long ago, contacts with the Arab world existed in the East African coastal region along the Indian Ocean, and from these emerged the Swahili culture, a blend of Arabic and African cultures that gave rise to the Swahili language widely spoken in East Africa today.

The Semitic culture of Ethiopia developed on the central plateau in northeastern Africa, and this differs from other Black African cultures in many ways. The Ethiopians grow an indigenous grain called *teff (Eragrostis abyssinica)*, and use its flour to make bread. More than one-third of the population are Coptic Christians, who have developed their own writing system. These two cultures, the Swahili and the Ethiopian, demonstrate the deep contact Black African cultures have had with those of both North Africa and West Asia. (Nobuyuki Hata)

A mosque in Jenne in the Republic of Mali.

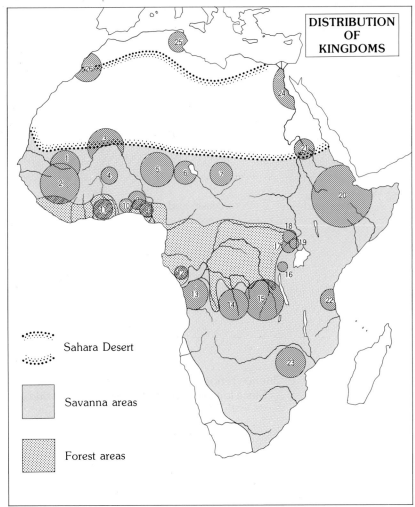

DISTRIBUTION OF KINGDOMS

Dates approximate the beginning of each kingdom.

1. Ghana (A.D. 1000)
2. Mali (A.D. 1325)
3. Songhay (A.D. 1500)
4. Mossi (A.D. 1450)
5. Hausa (A.D. 1400)
6. Bornu (A.D. 1600)
7. Wadai (A.D. 1635)
8. Benin (A.D. 1450)
9. Oyo (A.D. 1750)
10. Dahomey (A.D. 1800)
11. Ashanti (A.D. 1750)
12. Loango (A.D. 1500)
13. Congo (A.D. 1500)
14. Lunda (A.D. 1750)
15. Luba (A.D. 1500)
16. Ruanda (A.D. 1800)
17. Anchole (A.D. 1800)
18. Nyoro (A.D. 1800)
19. Buganda (A.D. 1800)
20. Ethiopia (A.D. 350)
21. Kush (700 B.C.)
22. Kilwa (A.D. 1400)
23. Monomotapa (A.D. 1475)
24. Egypt (1450 B.C.)
25. Carthage (300 B.C.)
26. Almoravid (A.D. 1075)

Sahara Desert

Savanna areas

Forest areas

A Bodi cattle-herder in the savanna of Ethiopia.

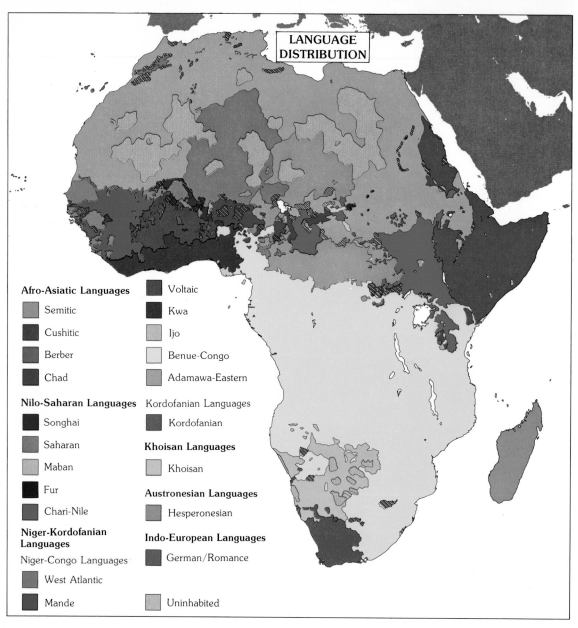

LANGUAGE DISTRIBUTION

Afro-Asiatic Languages
- Semitic
- Cushitic
- Berber
- Chad

- Voltaic
- Kwa
- Ijo
- Benue-Congo
- Adamawa-Eastern

Nilo-Saharan Languages
- Songhai
- Saharan
- Maban
- Fur
- Chari-Nile

Kordofanian Languages
- Kordofanian

Khoisan Languages
- Khoisan

Austronesian Languages
- Hesperonesian

Niger-Kordofanian Languages

Niger-Congo Languages
- West Atlantic
- Mande

Indo-European Languages
- German/Romance

- Uninhabited

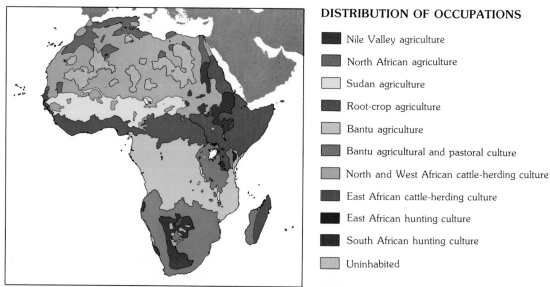

DISTRIBUTION OF OCCUPATIONS
- Nile Valley agriculture
- North African agriculture
- Sudan agriculture
- Root-crop agriculture
- Bantu agriculture
- Bantu agricultural and pastoral culture
- North and West African cattle-herding culture
- East African cattle-herding culture
- East African hunting culture
- South African hunting culture
- Uninhabited

The Course of African Civilization

Africa is the birthplace of the human race, and the history of the African peoples themselves began long before the appearance of written records. Rock paintings in the Sahara Desert and other places in Africa, archaeological artifacts, written documents, and oral history all bear witness to this. In medieval times, the savanna along the southern edge of the Sahara saw the rise and fall of Black African kingdoms such as Ghana and Mali. Trading cities flourished there, and Islam was introduced and spread. The coastal region of East Africa had strong connections with Persia and Arabia through trade via the Indian Ocean, and many city-states grew and developed there. In the forests of the Gulf of Guinea and the Congo basin were Black African kingdoms that worshiped sacred kings. Benin and Dahomey had contact with Europeans since the beginning of the sixteenth century, and both were severely damaged by the slave trade, which devastated African civilization and led to colonization by Europeans. From the 1960s, successive African nations have gained their independence, and today they are progressing toward a rebirth of the splendid cultures of the past.

❸ AH 0003

❶ AH 0016

 ❷ AH 0015

❶ **Gold Weights** (Guinea Coast, West Africa)
On the Guinea coast, long known as a center of the production of alluvial gold, sculpted weights were important in the gold trade.
❷ **Gold Weights** (Guinea Coast, West Africa)
These were developed for the alluvial gold trade both for weighing and setting trade prices.
❸ **Statue of Mother and Child** (The Ashanti, Ghana)
The motif of mother and child, symbolizing fertility, occurs widely in other societies as well.

❷ AH 0502

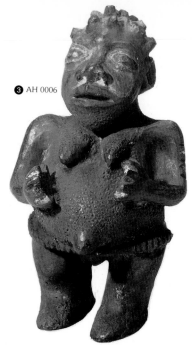

❸ AH 0006

❶ AH 0501

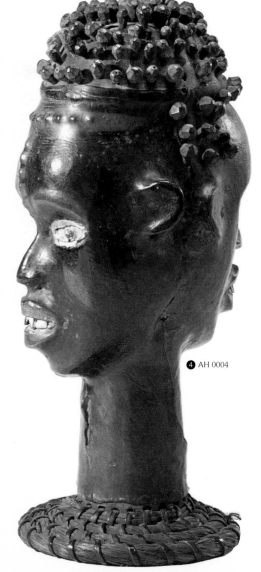

❶–❷ **Seated Figures** (Western Cameroon, Central Africa)
These brass figures portray a Bamun king and queen in traditional costume.
❸ **Clay Doll** (The Mambila, Nigeria)
This was used for magic, common in religious practices among African societies.
❹ **Two-faced, or Janus, Mask** (The Ekoi, Nigeria)
Common in African societies, masks symbolize mythical heroes and spirits associated with ancestor worship.
❺–❻ **Pipes** (Western Cameroon, Central Africa)
Pipes decorated with human figures were used by Bamun kings, and smoking was a symbol of kingship.

❺ AH 0495

❹ AH 0004

❻ AH 0496

The African Peoples and Their Ways of Life

Among the different societies found within Africa, there are some that have no central system of authority and others that have developed a monarchical system. Cattle-herding and fishing were rare, agriculture being the main means of livelihood, with the principal crops being grains and root vegetables. In agricultural techniques, these societies share many common aspects, such as the use of short-handled hoes and digging sticks, and the practice of grinding staple grains into flour and eating this in the form of dumplings. These societies also developed techniques for making iron farm implements and earthenware vessels. In the savanna, the nomads lived by herding cattle, goats, sheep, and camels, using their meat and milk. However, they had no earthenware vessels or iron farm tools; instead, they made containers from calabashes and wood, clothing and ornaments of leather, and spears and shields. Today, only a few people live by hunting and gathering. To make eating utensils and musical instruments, natural materials—calabashes, wood, and animal bones—are used, whereas metals requiring advanced technology, including bronze, are used for ornaments and ritual objects.

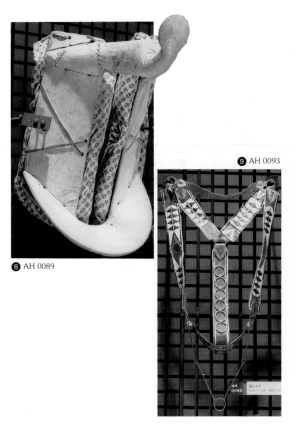

⑨ AH 0093

⑧ AH 0089

⑦ AH 0155, etc.

⑦ **Containers Used by Nomads**
Pastoral nomadic peoples use calabashes of various shapes for milking and storing sour milk. They are carried on leather belts and decorated with beads and cowrie shells. They are also used as food utensils for *ugari* (cereal gruel) and as water containers. In southwestern Ethiopia, bowls made of woven plant fibers are found.

⑧ **Saddle** (Northern Cameroon, Central Africa)
The wooden part of this horse saddle, typical of the southern edge of the Sahara in West Africa, is of wild date wood, and the leather part is of sheep- and goatskin.

⑨ **Horse Ornament** (Northern Cameroon, Central Africa)
Such head ornaments are made of sheep- and goatskin by saddlers.

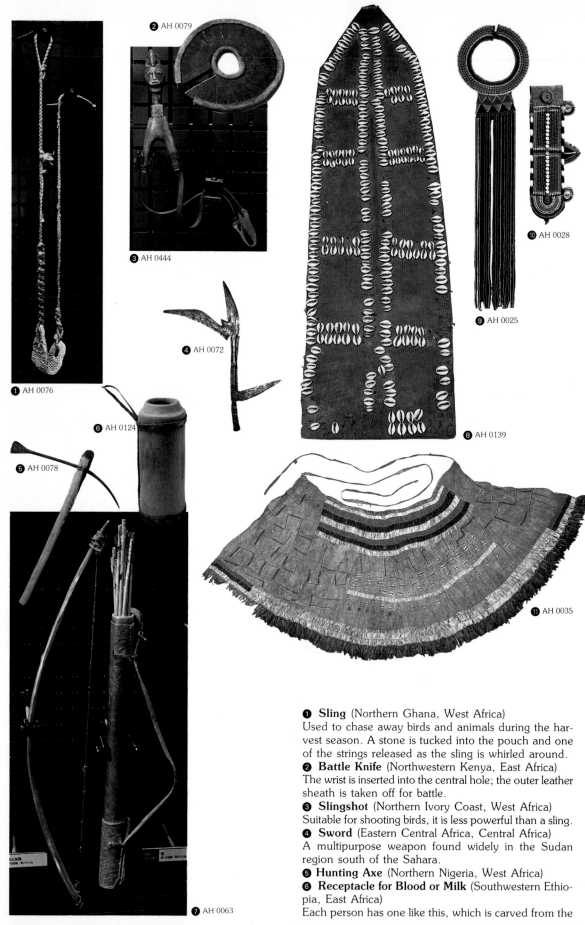

❷ AH 0079

❸ AH 0444

❿ AH 0028

❾ AH 0025

❹ AH 0072

❶ AH 0076

❽ AH 0139

❻ AH 0124

❺ AH 0078

⓫ AH 0035

❼ AH 0063

❶ **Sling** (Northern Ghana, West Africa)
Used to chase away birds and animals during the harvest season. A stone is tucked into the pouch and one of the strings released as the sling is whirled around.
❷ **Battle Knife** (Northwestern Kenya, East Africa)
The wrist is inserted into the central hole; the outer leather sheath is taken off for battle.
❸ **Slingshot** (Northern Ivory Coast, West Africa)
Suitable for shooting birds, it is less powerful than a sling.
❹ **Sword** (Eastern Central Africa, Central Africa)
A multipurpose weapon found widely in the Sudan region south of the Sahara.
❺ **Hunting Axe** (Northern Nigeria, West Africa)
❻ **Receptacle for Blood or Milk** (Southwestern Ethiopia, East Africa)
Each person has one like this, which is carved from the

wood of the *Anacardiaceae* tree, related to the lacquer tree.

❼ Bow and Quiver of Arrows (Northwestern Kenya, East Africa)
These were mainly used for hunting, rather than for battle, in the pastoral societies of East Africa.

❽ Woman's Ornament (Northern Kenya, East Africa)
Decorated with beads and cowrie shells, this is hung from the neck in front.

❾–❿ Bride's Necklace and Earring (Southern Kenya, East Africa)
Women's beaded ornaments that are worn in daily life are representative of the Masai and Samburu.

⓫ Ritual Skirt (Northern Tanzania, East Africa)
Of goatskin decorated with blue, white, and red beads,
such skirts were an important part of a bride's trousseau and evolved along with girls' coming-of-age ceremonies.

⓬–⓭ Lock and Pulley (⓬ Western Mali, West Africa; ⓭ Central Ivory Coast, West Africa)
Utilitarian but highly decorated. The pulley, which has the sheave missing, is used in weaving.

⓮ Hoes (Northern Tanzania, East Africa)
With characteristic short handles. People using them keep their knees straight and body bent at the waist, just employing the strength of their arms.

⓯ Wall-hanging (Central Benin, West Africa)
This ornament of appliquéd cloth tells the story of the historical kings of Dahomey, with each design representing an incident.

⓮ AH 0253, etc.

⓬ AH 0339

⓭ AH 0044

⓯ AH 0326

❶ AH 0168–0244

❷ AH 0185

④ AH 0411　　⑤ AH 0421　　⑥ AH 0419　　⑦ AH 0409

⑧ AH 0301–0307

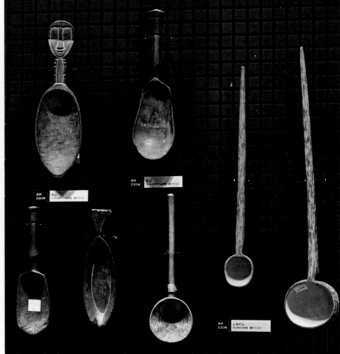

③ AH 0868

❶–❷ Calabashes (Northern Cameroon, Central Africa)
Calabashes, found widely in the savanna, are indispensable to the Fulbe people. The smaller calabashes are only used for decoration, and the larger ones for both decoration and as utensils. After the calabashes are colored, women use a hot knife to produce pyrographic designs.
❸ Earthenware Vessel (Northern Togo, West Africa)
Small and medium-sized pots are used for cooking and for water storage, and millet beer is brewed in the biggest ones, like this one.
❹–❼ Combs
Such large-toothed combs have carvings of people and animals.
❽ Wooden Ladles and Spoons

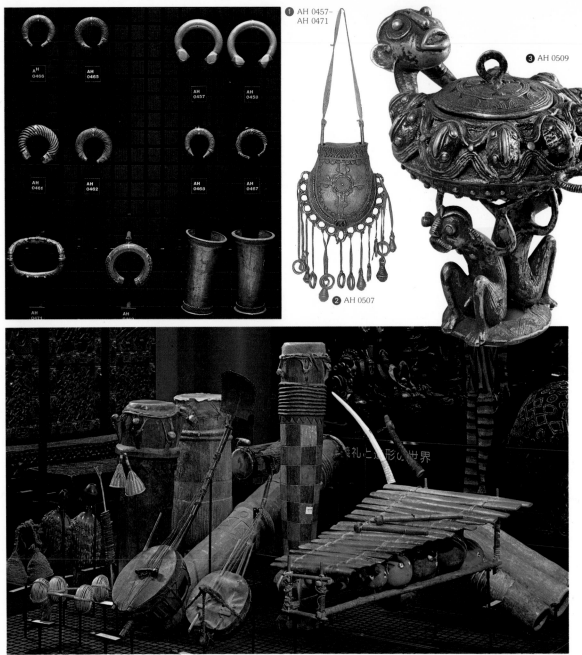

1 AH 0457–
AH 0471

3 AH 0509

2 AH 0507

礼と造形の世界

4 AH 0525, etc.

❶ Bracelets and Anklets (Northern Cameroon, Central Africa)
Metal bracelets and anklets found throughout West Africa were used as money and called *manila*.

❷ Purse (Northern Cameroon, Central Africa)
Used by the Kapsiki of the Mandara plateau. Its design reveals the influence of the cultures of the Sahara and the Maghreb areas.

❸ Soup Tureen (Western Cameroon, Central Africa)
This brass tureen is said to have been used by the Bamun king.

❹ Musical Instruments (West Africa)
These are mainly from the Baule people and include drums and rattle-like percussion instruments, tonal instruments such as balaphons (xylophones with calabash resonators under each slat) and *kora* (stringed instruments), and horns.

❺ Standing Screen (Western Cameroon, Central Africa)
This screen, called a *shup dap*, is placed behind the king of the Tikar during outdoor ceremonies. The upper part has carvings of scenes of life at the royal palace.

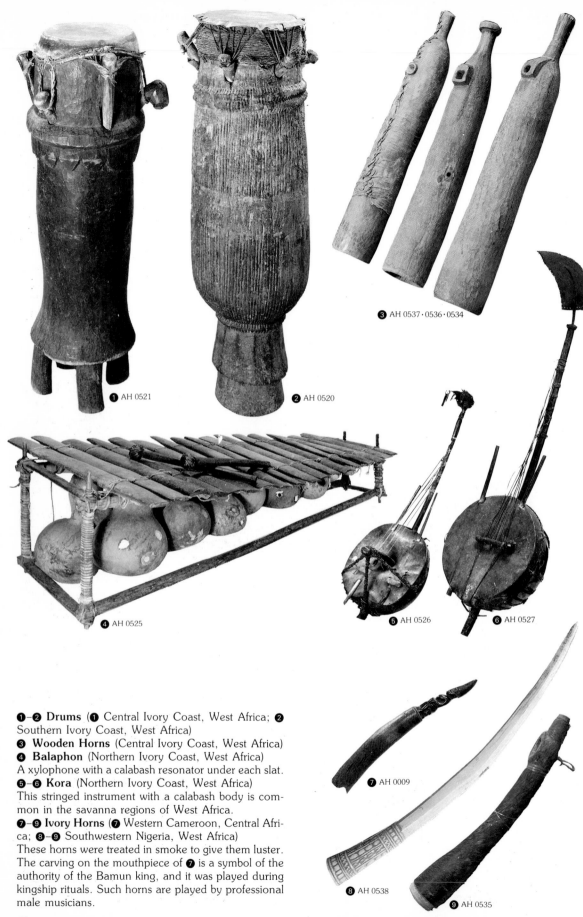

① AH 0521 **②** AH 0520

③ AH 0537 · 0536 · 0534

④ AH 0525

⑤ AH 0526 **⑥** AH 0527

⑦ AH 0009

⑧ AH 0538

⑨ AH 0535

①–② **Drums** (**①** Central Ivory Coast, West Africa; **②** Southern Ivory Coast, West Africa)
③ **Wooden Horns** (Central Ivory Coast, West Africa)
④ **Balaphon** (Northern Ivory Coast, West Africa)
A xylophone with a calabash resonator under each slat.
⑤–⑥ **Kora** (Northern Ivory Coast, West Africa)
This stringed instrument with a calabash body is common in the savanna regions of West Africa.
⑦–⑨ **Ivory Horns** (**⑦** Western Cameroon, Central Africa; **⑧–⑨** Southwestern Nigeria, West Africa)
These horns were treated in smoke to give them luster. The carving on the mouthpiece of **⑦** is a symbol of the authority of the Bamun king, and it was played during kingship rituals. Such horns are played by professional male musicians.

Rituals and the Plastic Arts

Black African history has been transmitted orally, and most sculptured figures commonly found from Central to West Africa symbolize ancestors and heroes of each ethnic group as they have been remembered over the generations. Religions are based on animism, the worship of natural objects, and on magic, and these beliefs have generated many idols and sculptures. Secret societies centering on these beliefs, as well as on sex or age, also exist, and masks and dances symbolizing them are a feature of rituals. The masks and sculptures represent the spiritual side of life, and their originality has brought them high acclaim as ethnic folk art and had a great influence on modern Western art. The increasing spread of Christianity and Islam in modern Africa has resulted in a decline in the production of these traditional arts. However, ritual musical instruments are still frequently used at such events as Christian church services, Independence Day parades, and evening gatherings.

⑩ **Figure** (The Ekoi, Nigeria)
This figure symbolizing Ekoi ancestors is used in burial ceremonies.
⑪ **Figure** (Zaire, Central Africa)
A ritual object covered with magical decorations, used by magicians of the Basonge.
⑫ **Coming-of-Age Ceremony Costumes** (Northern Zambia, East Africa)
These costumes, called *makishi*, were donned for dances at the ritual site for this ceremony and are common in African societies.

⑩ AH 0561

⑪ AH 0616

⑫ AH 0539–
AH 0543

67

❶ Sculpture (The Bobo, Burkina Faso)
The Bobo, known for the humor in their arts, make large wooden masks and small brass figures by the lost-wax method.

❷ Sculpture (The Senufo, Ivory Coast)
The sculptors are blacksmiths, and sculpting is closely connected with the rituals of a secret society called Poro.

❸ Sculpture (The Makonde, Southern Tanzania)
This "human pyramid" is of ebony, a wood rarely used in African sculpture.

❹ Sculptures (The Bamun, Western Cameroon)
These small brass dolls, called *mamba* in Bamun, are said to bring good luck to their owners.

❺ Mask (The Bakuba, Zaire)
Such decorative masks, made by professional artisans, represent the mythical progenitor of the people or of the chief's clan.

❶ AH 0588

❷ AH 0595

❸ AH 0612

❹ AH 0544–0560

❺ AH 0699

68

6 AH 0635

9 AH 0629

8 AH 0681

10 AH 0620

7 AH 0694

6 Mask (The Chan, Cameroon)
The masks of the Chan, who live on the plateaus in Cameroon, have exaggerated expressions.

7 Mask (The Man, Ivory Coast)
This mask is rare because it has a hand-woven cotton costume attached.

8 Mask (The Mende, Sierra Leone)
Most of the black wooden helmets of the secret society called Bundu are original designs by the sculptors.

9 Mask (The Bamileke, Cameroon)
The Bamileke are known for the use of sculpture in their architecture, and they are also skilled at beadwork, as shown here.

10 Mask (The Bamun, Cameroon)
A chief's mask with elaborate decoration on the upper part, this is called a *tuganga* and is used in dances and rituals.

The Life and Culture of the Coastal Swahili

Since long ago, the area bordering the Indian Ocean has had strong trade ties with Arabia, Persia, and India, and thus it developed differently from the interior regions. After the tenth century, the Omani Arabs moved to the area and established city-states in Zanzibar, Lamu, Mombasa, and Kilwa, and with the prosperity resulting from the Indian Ocean trade, a unique Swahili culture came to be developed, combining Arabian and African influences. The Swahili language used today in Tanzania, Kenya, and elsewhere is based on Bantu grammar and vocabulary, with the addition of Arabic, Persian, and Hindu loan words. The Swahili people are Muslims, and their lifestyle, including food, clothing, and dwellings, is strongly influenced by Arab-Islamic culture.

❷ AH 0719

❸ AH 0721

❶ **Chair** (Lamu Island, East Africa)
Such chairs with inlaid decoration were favored by rich merchants and were produced in the region of Lamu Island, which prospered from the Indian Ocean trade until the nineteenth century.

❷ **Tray** (Lamu Island, East Africa)
An example of traditional woodcraft that developed on the island, with Islamic influence evident in the carved patterns.

❸ **Noodle-maker** (Lamu Island, East Africa)
Noodles were introduced to limited areas of the Swahili region. When the handle of this implement is pushed down, the paste in the central part is squeezed out through holes in the bottom to form noodles.

❹–❺ **Horns** (Lamu Island, East Africa)
Made of ox horn and hollowed wood, these imitate ivory horns symbolizing kingship and are called *bembe* on the island.

❶ AH 0715

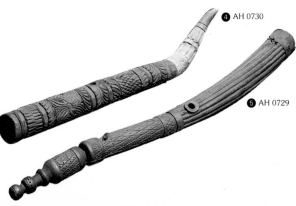

❹ AH 0730

❺ AH 0729

The Culture of Ethiopia

Ethiopia developed its own culture while maintaining close links with the cultures of West Asia, the Sudan area, and the ancient civilization of the Nile. Almost 100 different linguistic groups are in existence in Ethiopia, and they give great variety to its culture. The peoples speaking Amhara, Tigrinya, and Oroms of the Afro-Asiatic language group occupy the largest land area. The Ethiopian Orthodox Church, introduced in the fourth century, serves as the religious support of people on the central plateau, whose cuisine is characterized by its rich and spicy *injera*. Coffee-drinking originated in Ethiopia.

❻ Bible (Central Ethiopia, East Africa)
The canonical book of the Ethiopian Orthodox Church, hand-written in Ge'ez, the ancient Ethiopian ecclesiastical script. Such Bibles were carried by pilgrims.
❼ Carved Stone Tablets (Central Ethiopia, East Africa)
Each family has its own covenant tablets for worship.
❽ Lute (Central Ethiopia, East Africa)
This elegant multistringed lute called a *bägänd* developed among the upper classes and is usually placed on the floor and plucked with the fingernails.
❾–⓫ Utensils for Making Coffee
Traditional coffee-making utensils from Ethiopia, where coffee originated. Coffee beans are roasted in the pan (❾), ground in the mortar (❿), boiled in the clay pot (⓫), and the coffee drunk from small cups.

❽ AH 0750

❻ AH 0786

❾ AH 0745

❼ AH 0788

⓫ AH 0742

❿ AH 0747

❶ AH 0752–0780

❷ AH 0741

❶ **Crosses** (Central Ethiopia, East Africa)
These can be categorized into three types: those worn
by the clergy, those held in the right hand of priests, and
those used in ceremonial processions.
❷ **Table** (Central Ethiopia, East Africa)
This table is used for eating *injera*, made from the fermented flour of *teff*, a kind of grain cultivated only in
Ethiopia.

The Cultures of West Asia

The arid region of West Asia has nurtured the oldest civilizations of the world. Numerous groups of people intermingled here, cities were established from a very early date, and urban traditions have continued unbroken down to modern times. Many religions also originated in this area, but today Islam is the most extensive.

The structures of ethnic groups living in West Asia are exceedingly complex due to the numerous waves of migration that have swept across the region since antiquity. Four linguistic families are present here today: Indo-European, Caucasian, Altaic, and Afro-Asiatic (Hamito-Semitic). Indo-European languages are of the Armenian, Greek, Slavic, Albanian, and Indo-Iranian groups, and Indo-Iranian languages include Persian, Baluchi, Hazara, Pashtun, Tadzhik, and Kurd, speakers of which live mostly in or around Iran and Afghanistan. Armenian and Slavic languages are spoken mainly in the Soviet Union, Greek languages in Greece, and Albanian languages on the Balkan Peninsula. Small groups of speakers of some of these languages also exist in such places as Turkey and Iran.

Caucasian languages are concentrated around the Caucasus Mountains, with small groups of speakers also found in Syria and Turkey. Speakers of Altaic languages are descendants of the peoples who migrated west from the eastern regions of the Eurasian landmass. Uzbek, Turkmen, Azerbaijan, and Turkish, spoken in a belt that extends from Afghanistan to Iran, Turkey, and Syria, are evidence of that migration. The Afro-Asiatic language family is comprised of Berber, Cushitic, and Semitic languages, but it is the latter, including Arabic and Hebrew, that are most widely distributed in West Asia. Arabic is spoken in southern Iran, as well as in the Arab countries of Iraq, Syria, Jordan, and Saudi Arabia.

The arid region of West Asia is mostly located in the winter rain belt. Cultivation developed in ways adapted to local environments from around 9000 B.C., centering on wheat, barley, and beans. The flowering of man's oldest civilizations was a result of this agricultural abundance.

Since its formative period, West Asian agriculture has been closely linked to animal domestication, and sheep, goats, cattle, and camels were all raised for their milk, with cattle also being used for tilling and camels for transport. A nomadic pastoral lifestyle relying on animal domestication is a feature of mountainous regions and areas that are too dry for cultivation. "Agriculture and Animal Domestication" is the first theme of the West Asia exhibit.

The ancient civilizations that flourished due to agricultural plenty gave rise to many city-states, and West Asia is the site of the earliest cities in human history, so urban traditions have here been passed down for millennia. Thus, the second theme of the exhibit is "Urban Life."

West Asia is also the cradle of most of the world's great religions. Zoroastrianism, a prototype of the great religions, arose here about 700 B.C. Christianity and Judaism also developed in West Asia, and Islam took root here as well. At present, Islam is the predominant faith, and thus forms the third theme of the exhibit. (Masatake Matsubara)

AGE OF AGRICULTURAL SITES IN WEST ASIA
(measured by C-14 method)

Region	Site	B.C.	9000	8000	7000	6000	5000	4000	3000
Iran	Belt Cave					−	+		
	Bus Mordeh phase, etc.				+	−	+		
	Tepe Guran					−	+		
Iraq	Tepe Sarab					+			
	Jarmo				−				
	Zawi Chemi Shanidar		−						
	Matarrah						+		
Turkey	Çayönü Tepesi				+	−			
	Mersin					+			
	Çatal Hüyük				+				
Levant	Bouqras					− +			
	Ras Shamra					− −	+		
	Ramad					− +			
	Jericho			−	− −		+		
	Beldha			−					

+ Earthenware excavated
− Earthenware not excavated

74

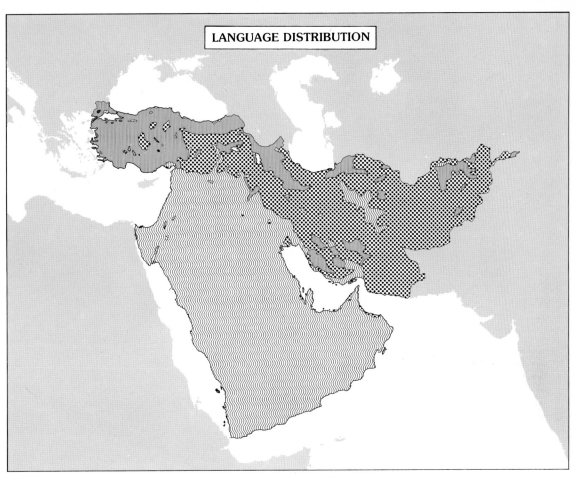

LANGUAGE DISTRIBUTION

Indo-European Languages

 Indo-Iranian

Armenian

Greek

Slavic

Albanian

Caucasian Languages

North Caucasian

Transcaucasian

Altaic Languages

Turkic

Afro-Asiatic (Hamito-Semitic) Languages

Semitic

Nomads in southern Iraq.

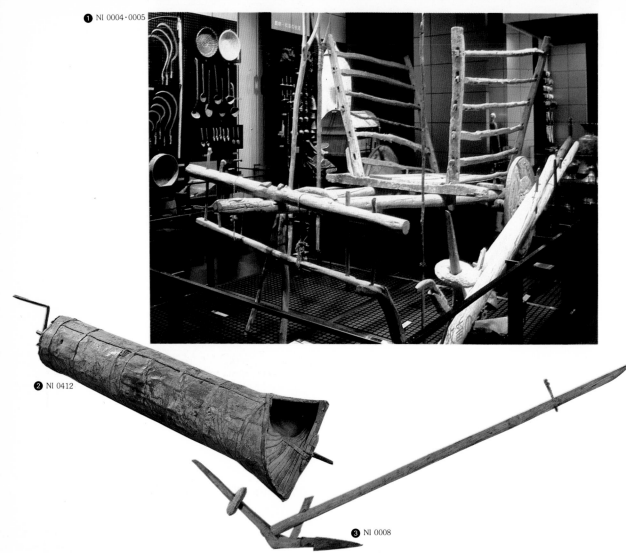

❶ NI 0004·0005

❷ NI 0412

❸ NI 0008

Agriculture and Animal Domestication

These means of livelihood are well suited to the dry regions of West Asia. Man first developed grain cultivation in the "fertile crescent," the region that runs along the Tigris and Euphrates rivers, and although early agriculture centered on crops like wheat and barley, a variety of beans and fruits were also important. Most West Asian cultivation depended on rain, but in some areas large-scale irrigation systems using underground channels (*kanāt* in Persian) and the like were constructed. Domesticated animals are mainly sheep, goats, cattle, camels, and horses, and bones of domesticated sheep and goats have been uncovered at agricultural sites in Iraq dating back nearly 10,000 years, proving that animal domestication is about as old as the cultivation of crops. Nomadic stock farming is found throughout West Asia, and in Afghanistan, Iran, and Turkey nomads move hundreds of kilometers between summer mountain sites and winter camps on the plains. The relationship between agriculture and stock farming has undergone numerous stages,

from the diversification of agriculture to the ultimate separation of the two, but the two ways of life are considered complementary.

❶ Ox Cart and Yoke (Burdur, Turkey)
This cart, pulled by a pair of oxen, is used for hauling dried grass or straw. The wheels are made of walnut and the axle of oak.
❷ Water Screw (Giza, Egypt)
Also called an Archimedes screw. Water is raised from canals when the screw is turned by either human or animal power.
❸ Plow (Burdur, Turkey)
Pulled by a pair of oxen. The depth of the soil to be turned can be altered by changing the stone, the position of the yoke, or the angle of the share tip to the shaft.
❹ Wheat Rakes (Burdur, Turkey)
Such rakes, made of willow or other wood, are held in the left hand to pull up toppled wheat stalks, which are then cut with a sickle held in the right hand.
❺ Finger Guards (Burdur, Turkey)
Worn on the four fingers of the left hand, these guards of wood such as peach and elm give protection when grain stalks are gathered in the left hand to be cut with a sickle held in the right.

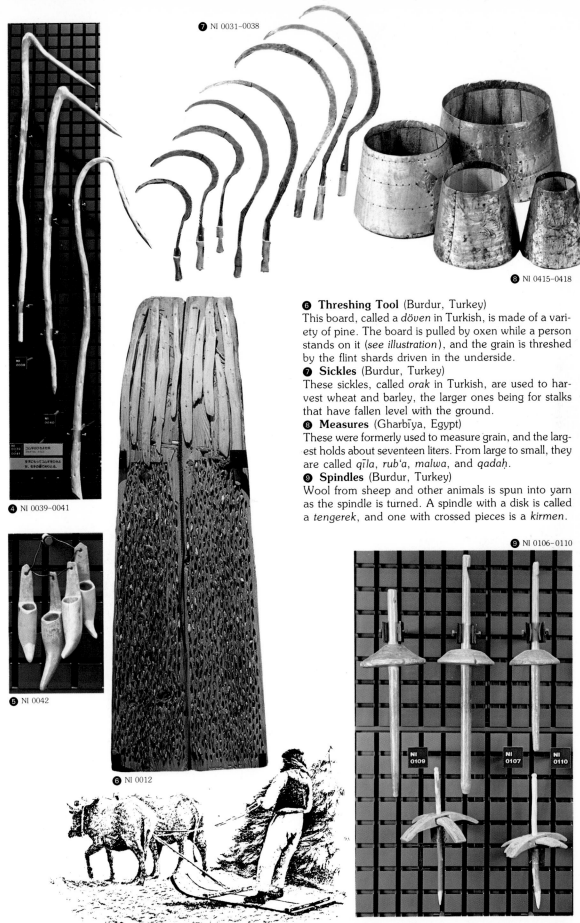

⑦ NI 0031–0038

⑧ NI 0415–0418

④ NI 0039–0041

⑤ NI 0042

⑥ NI 0012

⑥ Threshing Tool (Burdur, Turkey)
This board, called a *döven* in Turkish, is made of a variety of pine. The board is pulled by oxen while a person stands on it (*see illustration*), and the grain is threshed by the flint shards driven in the underside.

⑦ Sickles (Burdur, Turkey)
These sickles, called *orak* in Turkish, are used to harvest wheat and barley, the larger ones being for stalks that have fallen level with the ground.

⑧ Measures (Gharbīya, Egypt)
These were formerly used to measure grain, and the largest holds about seventeen liters. From large to small, they are called *qīla*, *rub'a*, *malwa*, and *qadaḥ*.

⑨ Spindles (Burdur, Turkey)
Wool from sheep and other animals is spun into yarn as the spindle is turned. A spindle with a disk is called a *tengerek*, and one with crossed pieces is a *kirmen*.

⑨ NI 0106–0110

77

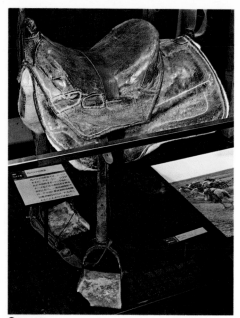

① NI 0080

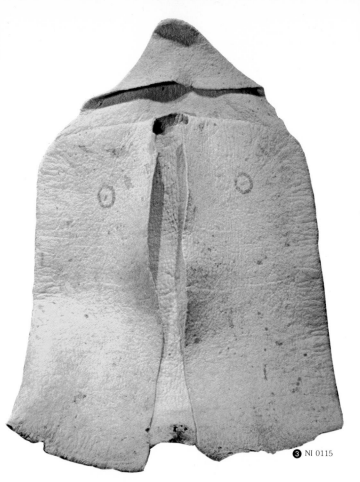

③ NI 0115

② NI 0419
NI 0420
NI 0421

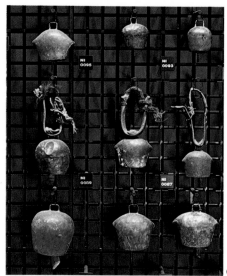

④ NI 0087, etc.

① **Saddle** (Burdur, Turkey)
Made from the skin of a male goat stretched over a wooden frame and stuffed with goat hair. The large stirrups are unusual.

② **Saddlebags** (Sharqīya, Egypt)
The top bag is used on a camel, those below on donkeys, both still important means of transport in rural villages.

③ **Felt Overcoat** (Burdur, Turkey)
Made of compressed sheep wool, this is draped over the shoulders for warmth and to keep the wearer dry, and it is also used when sleeping outdoors.

④ **Sheep Bells** (Burdur, Turkey)
About one in ten of a flock of sheep wears an appropriately sized bell around its neck, the sound of which tells the shepherd how far his flock has wandered.

Urban Life

From the earliest times, West Asia has come under the sway of many different groups of people, and this has resulted in sophisticated urban cultures. Cities with a history and cultural traditions going back several millennia are common, and Muslims, Christians, and Jews all live with their own traditions in contemporary urban societies. Most West Asian cities lie in arid regions where lifestyles are strongly influenced by the harsh natural environment, resulting in dwellings and clothing made with distinct materials, structures, functions, and forms. Social life in urban West Asia is centered on places of worship and the bazaar. Mosques serve not only a religious function but also play a vital political role, while the bazaar, or *sūq*, is the center of trade and of the production of arts and crafts and the implements of daily life. Most of the objects in the West Asia exhibit were made in or near a bazaar.

❺ **Rosewater Sprinklers** (Kuwait)
Throughout West Asia, water infused with the fragrance of roses is sprinkled over the heads of visitors in welcome, and it is also drunk.

❻ **Coffee Pot** (Najd, Saudi Arabia)
Peculiar to the Arabian Peninsula, this pot has a spout that can be closed. Coconut fibers serve as the filter.

❼ **Sherbet Ladle** (Iran)
Made of boxwood or pearwood, ladles may be decorated with relief and openwork designs from Iranian folk tales, traditional motifs such as the sun with lions and peacocks, and arabesques.

❽ **Hanging Lamps** (Isfahān, Iran)
Made of brass or copper, with geometric and arabesque openwork patterns.

❾ **Carpets** (*left*: Qum, Iran; *center*: Kabul, Afghanistan)
The silk carpet on the left depicts a hunting scene, and the center one is a typical Turkmen carpet with an octagonal motif.

❿ **Standing Screen** (Cairo, Egypt)
Traditional wooden latticework screen in the style called *mashrabīya* for the urban upper classes.

❺ NI 0525
NI 0526

❻ NI 0496

❼ NI 0531

❽ NI 0300·0299·0298

❾ NI 0295
NI 0297

❿ NI 0510

❶ NI 0191, etc.

❷ NI 0520

❸ NI 0521

❹ NI 0523

❶ Clothing
The general purpose of clothing is to protect the wearer from the elements, which in West Asia means protection from the sun and sandstorms, and for the sake of modesty. Both men and women wear garments that cover the body from head to foot.

❷–❸ Water Pipes (❷ Jidda, Saudi Arabia; ❸ Cairo, Egypt)
Water-filtered tobacco smoke is enjoyed throughout the region, although the shape of smoking implements varies from place to place.

❹ Pillow (Kuwait)
Used for leaning one's elbow on or for sleeping, this *masnad* is found in all Arab living rooms.

❺ Caps
Worn in various areas of Egypt, Turkey, Iraq, Iran, and Afghanistan, usually under a turban. Each cap's design represents the group to which the wearer belongs and is thus a means of identification.

❻ Panel of Tiles (Isfahān, Iran)
An early twentieth-century wall decoration depicting a traditional hunting scene.

❼–❽ Pen Cases (Shīrāz, Iran)
Made of papier-mâché, decorated with pigment, and lacquered, a style popular in the nineteenth and early twentieth centuries.

❾ Painted Ceiling (Shīrāz, Iran)
Painted in the nineteenth century on the ceiling of a mansion, this shows the strong European influence of the period.

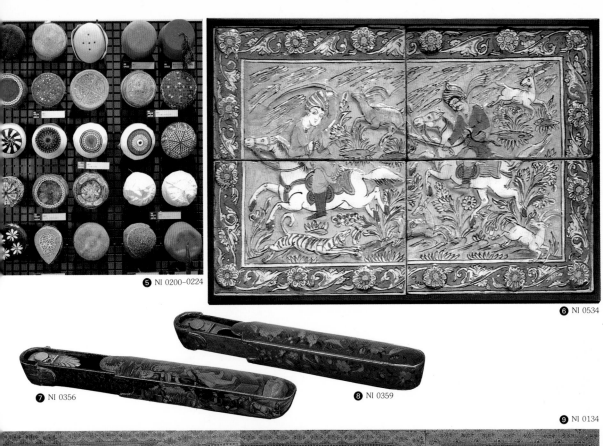

❺ NI 0200–0224

❻ NI 0534

❼ NI 0356

❽ NI 0359

❾ NI 0134

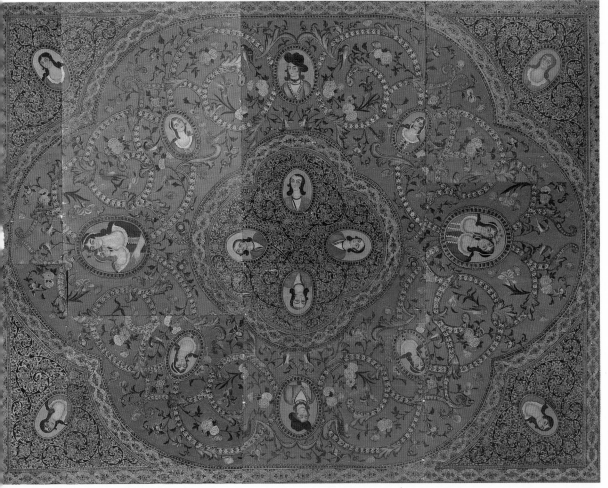

❶ NI 0513
❷ NI 0490
❸ NI 0505

❹ NI 0323
❺ NI 0324
❻ NI 0456

❼ NI 0452, etc.

❽ NI 0447

❶ **Small Table** (Damascus, Syria)
Made in the nineteenth century and inlaid with bone, ivory, and mother-of-pearl.

❷ **Brazier** (Aleppo, Syria)
Charcoal was burned for warmth in this late eighteenth-century brass brazier.

❸ **Shadow Puppet** (Istanbul, Turkey)
Karagöz ("Dark Eye") is both the hero and the vernacular name of the shadow-puppet theater. Sticks are pushed into holes in such camel-skin puppets, which are then manipulated behind a curtain.

❹–❺ **Water Pitcher and Basin** (Kandahar, Afghanistan)
Such copper pitchers for washing the hands and rinsing the mouth before and after meals are usually paired with a basin for catching the water.

❻ **Anklet** (Najd, Saudi Arabia)
An anklet with a clasp at the central coin. Anklets with bells are used in dances.

❼ **Accessories**
Greco-Roman, Syrian, Egyptian, and Sāsānian jewelry techniques spread throughout the Islamic world. The Prophet Muhammad forbade ostentation, and thus comparatively inexpensive silver articles are preferred.

❽ **Necklace** ('Asīr, Saudi Arabia)
The hexagonal portion of this accessory, which also serves as a talisman, can hold a small Qur'ān.

The World of Islam

Islam, a faith that first evolved in West Asia, has numerous elements in common with Christianity and Judaism, both of which preceded it historically. Islam began in the early seventh century with Muhammad's revelations in the town of Mecca on the Arabian Peninsula, in what is now western Saudi Arabia. In less than a century, it had spread east to Persia and as far west as North Africa and the Iberian Peninsula. From the nineteenth century, Islam was greatly affected by colonialism and modernization, but today it is a vigorous religion followed by most people in West Asia and has a strong influence on their societies. According to basic Islamic teachings, believers must submit absolutely to Allah, the one and only God, and thus they are firmly against polytheism. Sacred images and pictures are forbidden, and there is no deification of Muhammad himself. The basic tenets of Islam are contained in six beliefs—belief in Allah, the Angels, the Qur'ān, the Prophets, the Day of Judgment, and Destiny—and five practices—the profession of faith, the performance of daily prayers, fasting during the month of Ramaḍān, almsgiving, and making a pilgrimage to Mecca. The Sunnī and the Shī'a are the two main sects of Islam, the Sunnī being the larger. Members of the Shī'a sect are found mostly in Iraq, Iran, and other countries bordering the Persian Gulf.

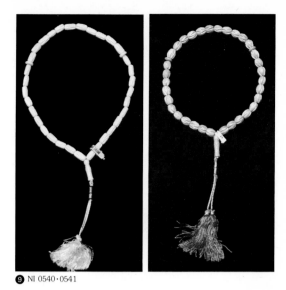

⑨ NI 0540·0541

⑩ NI 0365
NI 0362

⑪ NI 0538

⑫ NI 0369–0371

⑨ **Strings of Beads** (Dubai, United Arab Emirates)
Used as a tally when chanting the ninety-nine names of Allah, such strings usually contain thirty-three beads.
⑩ **Qur'ān and Stand** (Tehrān, Iran; Kabul, Afghanistan)
This Qur'ān was copied in the Islamic year A.H. 1153 (A.D. 1740). The cover is of goatskin, and the pages are decorated with gold leaf.

⑪ **Qur'ān Cabinet** (Cairo, Egypt)
Of brass with gold and silver inlay, this was produced in the nineteenth century in the style of the Mamlūk dynasty (l3th–l6th centuries).
⑫ **Alms Bowls** (Tehrān, Iran)
These *kashkūl* of metal or coco-de-mer shell are carried by dervishes, or wandering mystics.

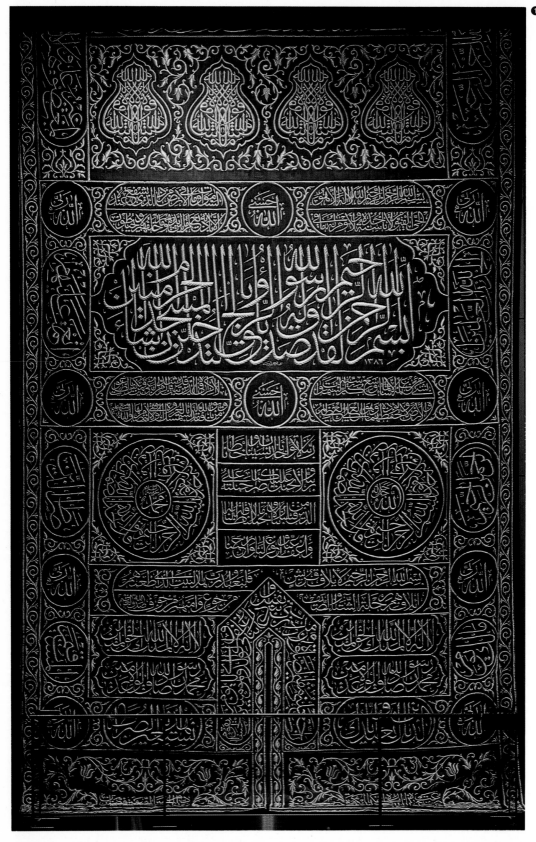

❶ Covering of the Ka'aba Shrine (Mecca, Saudi Arabia)
This section of cloth with verses from the Qur'ān embroidered in gold and silver thread is part of the Kiswa, the black silk cloth that covers the Ka'aba, the small shrine located in the center of the Sacred Mosque in Mecca, the most sacred place in the world for Muslims. The Kiswa is replaced each year during the pilgrimage period.

Music

Music is an essential element in peoples' lives, and the many ethnic groups in the world are blessed with music brimming with vitality and permeated with pathos and delicacy—a manifestation of the joy of life itself. Ethnic music can in no way be considered inferior to the European music that developed over the last few centuries.

Despite the fact that many types of music exist among the world's ethnic groups, this music has only recently begun to attract interest because of the long-established dominance of a monolithic theory of musical evolution that suggested European music was the standard and goal toward which all music should strive. In the past, it was believed that all musical systems which differed from the European tradition were backward and undeveloped, and that as the various societies progressed, their music would come to resemble European music. Even in Japan, European music has been the basis of musical education since the beginning of the Meiji period in 1868, and, because of this, scant attention was paid to traditional or ethnic Japanese music, or the music of other non-European groups.

Current interest in ethnic music addresses all the musical expressions of different ethnic groups without attempting to discriminate between them or rank them. It seeks to understand the meaning and structure of music, as well as to comprehend the culture and characteristics of each ethnic group through its music. The comparative study of music of different ethnic groups is called ethnomusicology, or musical anthropology. Before World War II, this field was called comparative musicology, because research at that time focused on comparisons of various types of ethnic music using European music as the standard, and it was concerned mainly with the analysis of musical structure.

In recent years, however, the study of music as one aspect of ethnic culture has begun to emerge, and music is seen as a form of human behavior and a value system. The attempt is now being made to study music within its social and cultural context, addressing not only traditional music and that of small ethnic groups but encompassing all forms of music in social and ethnic groups and seeking to understand such issues as the meaning and function of music, its social role and background, and its structure. This does not simply extend to what is already recognizable as music or musical expression, for the field of ethnomusicology also covers the relationship between sound and groups of people, since sound is the basic unit of music and existed before musical expression came into being.

Sounds exist everywhere and are related to lifestyles. Both the perception of sound and the sense of hearing can be regarded as culturally defined abilities, and thus sound is closely connected with civilization. The ear is more than an auditory organ because, through social interaction, it develops the capacity to make judgments—in other words, it possesses a cultural ability. The sounds of nature and of daily life are perceived and selected according to certain criteria, and are paired with performance and ritual to become "cultural sounds," that is, music. Thus, the sounds that form the basis of music express a group's feelings and inclinations, and they display great variety depending on climate, social structure, culture, and religion. Some groups of people may prefer high sounds, others low; some feel more comfortable with soft sounds, others enjoy sharp or blurred sounds. The analysis and comparison of the perception of these sounds within their cultural contexts is the new focus of ethnomusicology.

This exhibit concentrates on the ethnic music of Asia, which is closely related to Japanese ethnic music. The vast continent of Asia has produced a wide variety of cultures—among them nomadic societies in arid lands and societies centering around rice cultivation in wet regions—and this variety is a consequence of different racial and linguistic groups, as well as distinct religions, such as Islam, Hinduism, and Buddhism. Consequently, the music of Asia manifests an enormous variety; in other words, the predilections and feelings of a great number of peoples have produced the infinite diversity of Asian music. However, we can divide the music of Asia by geographical area into separate cultural spheres that have certain elements in common, such as musical structure, instruments, social function, and historical background.

The first cultural sphere is East Asia, which encompasses Japan, the Korean Peninsula, and most of continental China. Historically, of course, there has been much interchange between these areas, and their music shares certain characteristics and structural elements and employs similar instruments. In the Southeast Asian sphere, there are some cultural differences between the mainland areas and the nearby islands, but the region is linked by the *Ramayana* dance-drama, which is performed throughout the area and has resulted in shared elements of musical culture.

South Asia, centered in the Indo-Asian continent, is a world that revolves around Hinduism, and it has produced Indian classical music and precise musical theory that reached an advanced level even in ancient times. Yet the many ethnic groups in the area also reveal a rich musical diversity. Afghanistan and the cultures of the West Asian sphere have experienced complex interactions with other folk music since long ago, and in the Middle Ages this region achieved a brilliant musical culture. Shared elements in the ethnic music of the cultures there relate to the area's highly developed tradition of musical artistry, its societies that evolved in arid climates, and the Islamic religion.

Music from the Central Asian sphere shares many features with West Asian music, but it has been influenced by the cultures of North Asia and the Mongols to produce a singular musical grouping. Among common musical elements in this region, which encompasses Mongolia and Tibet, are musical structure, the way folk songs are sung, and the instruments themselves. (Tomoaki Fujii)

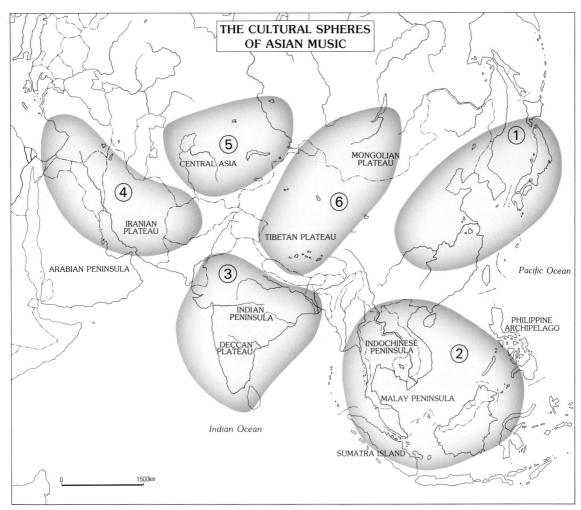

THE CULTURAL SPHERES OF ASIAN MUSIC

① East Asian sphere   ② Southeast Asian sphere   ③ Indian sphere   ④ West Asian sphere   ⑤ Central Asian sphere
⑥ Mongolian and Tibetan sphere

Musical Instruments

With a few exceptions, such as the aboriginal Veddas of Sri Lanka, people throughout the world play musical instruments, and these are closely related to everyday life and fulfill a variety of functions, beginning with religious rituals. In one sense, musical instruments transcend their function of producing sound to become cultural and ethnic symbols. In many groups, musical instruments are treated as symbols of people or animals and are given human or animal names, or their parts are named af-

2 ON 0016

3 ON 0015

❶ ON 0064–
ON 0117

ter parts of the human body. And many cases are found where instruments are treated as symbols of religious ceremonies or of authority. Great diversity is found in the materials, structure, shape, and methods of tuning and playing instruments in different ethnic groups. Traditionally, instruments were categorized as belonging to either the string, wind, or percussion groups, but they are now being classified according to how the sound is produced, leading to such divisions as plucked, blown, struck, and scraped instruments.

❶ Gamelan Ensemble (Jogjakarta, Indonesia)
The Indonesian *gamelan* is an ensemble of melodic metal percussive instruments that produces a sophisticated music. Although the *gamelan* on the islands of Java and Bali, where this traditional music is still extant, have many similarities, there are some differences in the names and types of instruments and in musical expression. However, the *gamelan* of both islands achieve a superb synthesis

of the many instruments to create music of great delicacy.
❷–❹ Indian Instruments (Delhi, India)
Classical Indian music can be divided into two types: Hindustani music of northern India, and Karnatic music of the south. With the spread of Islam into northern India, Hindustani music has been influenced by Arab and other music from the west, while Karnatic music still preserves ancient musical traditions.

❹ ON 0014

❶–❹ Korean Instruments (Sŏul, Korea)
From long ago, Korean music was strongly influenced by Chinese music, but it has its own performance characteristics, including its own rhythmical structure. Many of the great variety of instruments found in Korea are related to those of China and Japan.

❺–❼ Afghani Instruments (Kabul, Afghanistan)
Afghanistan has been called the "crossroads of civilization," and this is exemplified in its unique music, which developed under the constant influence of neighboring regions such as India, Iran, and Central Asia. Among the many types of instruments found there, the category of plucked instruments is especially rich, and these are usually beautifully decorated.

❽–❿ Iranian Instruments (Tehrān, Iran)
Iran has maintained an outstanding musical tradition since ancient times. In the Middle Ages, the music became inextricably mixed with Arab, Turkish, and other influences, resulting in music of a high cultural level. This ensemble of three instruments—the *dombaq* (❿; a pot-shaped, single-sided drum), the tamborine-like *def* (❽), and the *kemanche* (❾; a plucked instrument also played with a bow)—is used in both folk and classical music.

❶ ON 0020
❷ ON 0021
❸ ON 0026
❹ ON 0023
❺ ON 0011
❻ ON 0007
❼ ON 0008
❽ ON 0005
❾ ON 0004
❿ ON 0003

Japanese Instruments

In either classical or folk performing arts, the musical instruments most frequently found in Japan are the flute and drum, both of which have deep roots in the music of Japan. Many types of these instruments developed for different uses. The flute plays a simple melody, while the drum emphasizes the rhythm and is related to the concept of *ma* (an interval of time), which is distinctive in Japanese music. The *sô* (*koto*) and the *syamisen* are plucked instruments that have now become well known outside Japan, but there are other plucked instruments as well, such as the *kokyû* and the *biwa*, which are also found throughout the East Asian region. The *sô* was originally Chinese, but the *syamisen*, *kokyû*, and *biwa* can be traced to West Asia. After their introduction to China, these instruments were modified by the Chinese and brought to Japan and modified further. Besides the well-known *syakuhati*, other Japanese blown instruments include the *hitiriki* and the *syô*, both of which are used in the classical court music and dance called *gagaku*. All are of Chinese origin, although instruments of the same family as the *syakuhati* and *hitiriki* are also found in West Asia and Arabia. Instruments related to the *syô* are found only in East and Southeast Asia. The dramatic effect of Kabuki performances is heightened by the use of many devices that produce sounds.

⑪ Kokyû

A three- or four-stringed instrument played with a bow, which was used in ensembles of three in the Edo period (1603–1867) but has virtually disappeared since then.

⑫ Syamisen

This entered Japan from China by way of Okinawa, and has been widely used since the Edo period to accompany singing and storytelling.

⑬–⑰ Drums

One characteristic of Japanese drums is that almost all are double-headed, with skins stretched across both ends of the body.

⑱–㉙ Instruments for Kabuki Music

The musical accompaniment to Kabuki drama is called *hayasi* or *geza* music. If we include the *syamisen* (which accompanies *nagauta*, or dramatic chanting), the flute, and the drum, as well as the devices used to produce various sound effects, as many as fifty types of instruments are used in Kabuki.

㉚ Sô

This instrument, also called the *koto*, usually has thirteen strings today.

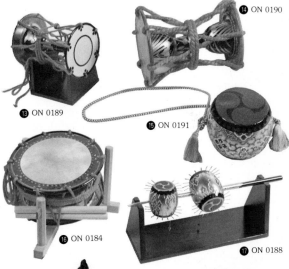

⑬ ON 0189
⑭ ON 0190
⑮ ON 0191
⑯ ON 0184
⑰ ON 0188

⑱ ON 0156
⑲ ON 0153
⑳ ON 0155
㉑ ON 0161
㉒ ON 0148
㉓ ON 0142
㉔ ON 0162
㉕ ON 0144
㉖ ON 0146
㉗ ON 0170
㉘ ON 0152
㉙ ON 0149
⑪ ON 0194
⑫ ON 0193
㉚ ON 0192

① ON 0119-0138・0403・0404

② ON 0132

③ ON 0138

④ ON 0400・0401

❶ Gagaku Instruments

Chinese music entered Japan from the fifth and sixth centuries, and an ancient indigenous form of Japanese dance was added to this to produce the court music called *gagaku*. *Gagaku* instruments show the strong influence of Tang-dynasty China in their types and shapes as well as in their decorative colors and designs.

❷ Syô

Also called a *hôsyô*, this is an instrument used only in *gagaku*. Sound is produced when air is blown through the mouthpiece, making the reeds at the base of the seventeen thin bamboo pipes vibrate.

❸ Hitiriki

A vertical flute used in *gagaku*. There are seven holes in front and two at the back. Despite its small size, it produces a loud sound when the two reeds vibrate. The *hitiriki* is thought to have been brought to Japan from West Asia through China.

❹ Dadaiko

There are two types of this, the largest of the drums used in *gagaku*: one is used for Chinese-style music, the other for Korean-style music. Each drum has different decoration and colors.

無垢淨經
相輪陀羅尼
卷一引薩婆怛
他揭多毗盧
羅曳下移勲天
憝撒下竹九圖
二五
未尼羯誘迦
畢生昌制折
哆三毗菩瑟
哆曳琵檄四
杜瑟杜普五
三昜哆眺眥
吉帝大雀羅
薩羅播骏翰
達尼七苦遠
尼三苦達尼
八鉾羅上戈
羅上曳琵檄
扰羅丸未尼
脱搭十鹅眥
止羅上未羅
毗戒第十咩
引牛裝引�

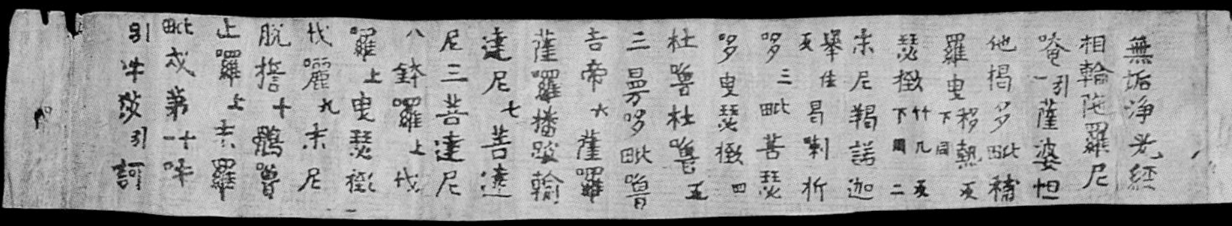

Language

Language is the key to culture, and every word may be thought of as a repository of cultural elements, whose content is expressed in the form of sounds that are subsequently transposed into written characters. In this way, barriers of time and space are breached, and language becomes the most important means of extending the boundaries of communication, facilitating communal living, and accumulating the fruits of the human intellect.

Language is the most palpable means of distinguishing between peoples, and a common language is a precondition for the development of a people's consciousness. Conversely, a person is only too conscious of the inability to communicate with someone who speaks a different language. For these reasons, the recognition of a national language is often one of the conditions for a people's independence.

The distribution of racial groups around the world is essentially the same as the distribution of languages, although there are a few exceptions such as Bulgaria, where the people speak a Slavic language but are Altaic in origin. Thus, it is inconceivable to compile a map of racial distribution without first mapping out language distribution. In cases where language and racial group do not coincide, only a detailed study of that group's history can reveal this. Hence, language is the first means of distinguishing between groups of people.

On making contact with a group of people and interacting with them, an understanding of their language is essential to an understanding of their ways of thought, because the values inherent in their lives are reflected in, and can only be comprehended through, their language. An ignorance of those

values often results in culture shock and misunderstanding. In this way, language is both a means for conveying information and the best tool for understanding a people's spirit.

Words that name things and facts provide the easiest means of learning about a group's culture, for they are repositories of cultural data. In any given vocabulary, the existence of a large number of words relating to something particular indicates its importance in the lives of the people speaking that language. For example, the wealth of Japanese words relating to rain and fish, or Arabic words dealing with camels, or Eskimo expressions connected with snow reveals elements in their environments of particular concern to those peoples.

The values and world view of a group of people are also clearly expressed in the unique systems of classification that exist in the language, such as kinship terms and terms for domestic animals, illnesses, and the like. This sort of classification occurs in all languages, and thus, as an itemized index of culture, vocabulary is one key to the study of groups of people.

As language given visual form, writing is easy to comprehend, but it is not language *per se*: spoken language is the original form and it long predated

FAMILIES OF WRITING SYSTEMS

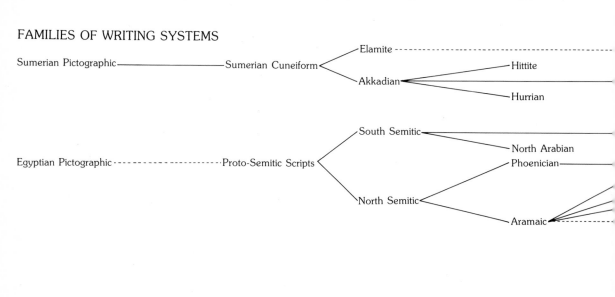

Compiled from I. J. Gelb, *A Study of Writing* (London, 1952); T. Nishida, *Sekai no moji* (Tokyo, 1981); and A. Gaur, *A History of Writing* (London, 1984).

writing in the history of humanity. Even today, languages exist in every part of the world that do not yet have any written forms. Most writing systems developed in advanced civilizations, and were then adopted or copied by other groups, and in the process were adapted to the languages of those groups.

As a rule, families of writing systems are not related to families of languages; for example, even though the same Arabic script is used, the Persian and Arabic languages belong to completely different linguistic groups. Nevertheless, written language is as important as spoken language in providing information for learning about different groups of people and for learning the history of cultural interchange. Languages are generally classified by family, but they can also be classified by type, which helps us understand the universality as well as the various patterns of human language.

The Language exhibit includes a section on written language and a technical display. The former traces the creation and development of writing systems, and the latter is concerned with sound production and word order. The display includes recordings of a folk tale in various Japanese dialects, an examination of the relationship between types of spoken sounds and the anatomical parts that are used to produce them, and spoken and written examples of word order in languages around the world. These participatory displays are designed to allow the visitor to "see" as well as to hear the characteristics of language. (Yuiti Wada)

THREE-DIMENSIONAL DIAGRAM OF VOWEL SOUNDS

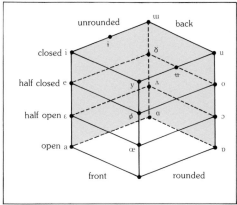

- - - - - - - - - - Old Persian

———————— Urartian

———————————— Ethiopic

———Greek———Contemporary European Scripts
———Nabatean————————— Arabic
ac
————————— Square Hebrew
——Indian Scripts————South and Southeast
——Central Asian Scripts   Asian Scripts

Japanese (Kana)
Khitan
Xixia
Jurchen
Korean
Modern Chinese
Vietnamese
Ancient Moso
Lolo

LIP CONFIGURATIONS

[ʉ]	[y]
[ɸ]	[œ]
[i]	[ɨ]
[u]	[ɯ]
[a]	[ɑ]
[o]	[ɔ]
[e]	[ɛ]

WORLD LINGUISTIC MAP

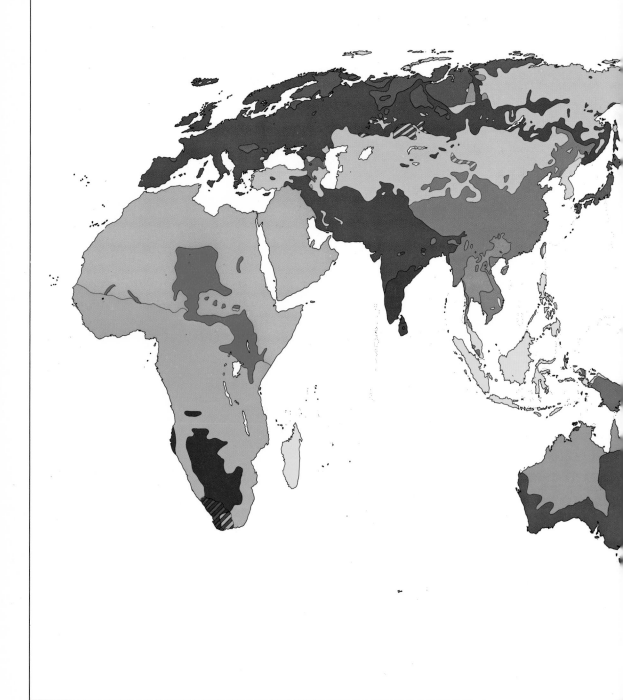

Indo-European Languages

Basque

Caucasian Languages

Uralic Languages

Altaic Languages

Ket

Korean

Ainu

Japanese

Sino-Tibetan Languages

Dravidian Languages

Austro-Asiatic Languages

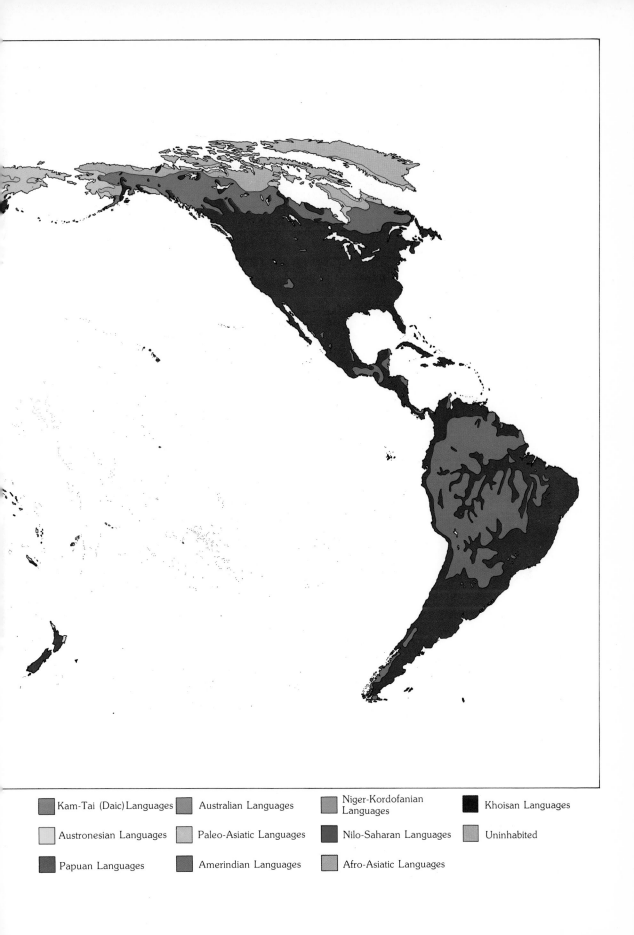

Kam-Tai (Daic)Languages

Austronesian Languages

Papuan Languages

Australian Languages

Paleo-Asiatic Languages

Amerindian Languages

Niger-Kordofanian
Languages

Nilo-Saharan Languages

Afro-Asiatic Languages

Khoisan Languages

Uninhabited

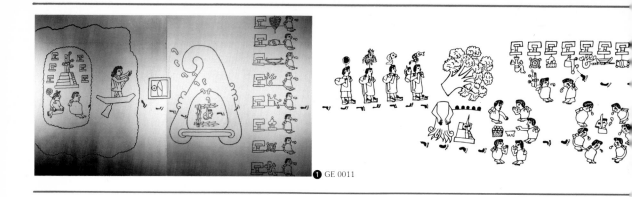

❶ GE 0011

❷ GE 0087

❸ GE 0003

❹ GE 0001

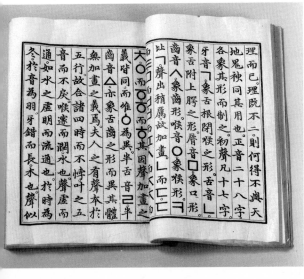

① Pictorial Record of a Tribal Migration (reproduction) (The Aztecs, Mexico)

This retains the character of a picture while displaying the first signs of stylization and meaning, and, as such, it suggests the shift from pictures to writing. The panels on the wall in the display area show the first tenth of the story of the migration of the Aztecs, which goes as follows: "Eight tribes left the Land of Seven Caves in A.D. 1116 and worshiped the god of war beside a tree. The god became angry, however, and destroyed the tree, and the tribespeople were scattered in all directions. The Aztecs were defeated in battle at a river delta and were taken captive, but they helped their captors fight other enemies, collecting the ears of those they killed as proof of their loyalty, and continued to wander." The object over the head of each figure is his or her tribe's name. The calendar portion of the story has been omitted.

② The Rosetta Stone (replica) (Egypt)

Named after the place where it was found, near the mouth of the Nile, this stone has a eulogy to Ptolemy inscribed in three scripts (Greek with hieroglyphic and demotic translations). It was deciphered by Jean-François Champollion (1790–1832), enabling Egyptian hieroglyphs to be read.

③ Rubbing from Duke Mao's Tripod (reproduction) (China)

Dating to the late Western Zhou dynasty (827–782 B.C.), this rubbing is of the writing carved inside a bronze tripod, the longest inscription (497 characters) on a bronze vessel in existence.

④ Tablets from an Inner Wall of a Checkpoint (reproduction) (Juyongguan, Hebei Province, China)

On these tablets from the checkpoint at Juyongguan, about 400 kilometers north-northwest of Beijing, a Buddhist sutra is carved in six different scripts (Xixia or Tangut, Uighurian, Mongolian, Tibetan, Lantsa-nagari Sanskrit, and Chinese). The large characters give the sounds of the sutra in Sanskrit, and the small characters give its translation. The tablets thus provide the key to reading these different scripts, and they are comparable in importance to the Rosetta Stone in the West.

⑤ The Hunmin Chŏngŭm (reproduction) (Korea)

This is a copy of the book that introduced *hangŭl*, the Korean alphabet. *Hangŭl* is not a pictographic script but a phonetic alphabet based on the shapes of the speech organs. It was conceived in 1443 by the fourth king of the Li dynasty of Korea and officially introduced in 1446.

⑤ GE 0085

❶ GE 0005

❸ GE 0002

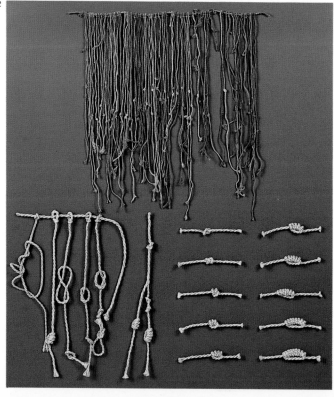

❶ **Memorial Tablet** (replica) (New Kingdom of Ancient Egypt)
With Egyptian pictographs carved in limestone.
❷ **The Gutenberg Bible** (reproduction) (Germany)
Printed by Johannes Gutenberg between 1450 and 1455, this is the oldest text printed with movable type.

❸ **Incan Knotted Ropes** (replicas) (Peru)
The ropes in the top row are replicas of Incan knotted ropes dating to about the sixteenth century and used to record or communicate information, for which color played a significant role. The ropes at the bottom right express numbers.

The Cultures of Southeast Asia

Rice forms the mainstay of life among the peoples of Southeast Asia, and many different culti-vation techniques flourish in the region and are reflected in colorful local lifestyles. Arts and crafts that have developed over the centuries continue to thrive throughout the area, and the harmonious blend of indigenous and foreign cultures is evident in the region's rich and varied art forms.

As a region, Southeast Asia is characterized by unity amid diversity. Geographically, it manifests great variety, from continental to insular and from mountainous to flat. The languages spoken by the peoples who live there are classified into a number of groups, as shown in the map. As a whole, Southeast Asia falls within the subtropical and tropical zones influenced by monsoons, allowing the extensive cultivation of paddy fields that results in the predominance of societies and cultures centered around rice cultivation.

The primary theme of the Southeast Asia exhibit is rice cultivation and its accompanying cultural aspects. People till the land, plant, harvest, and store rice, and various techniques employing a wide range of tools and facilities have been developed for this process.

In the lowlands of Southeast Asia, the principal paddy cultivators, such as the Vietnamese, the Khmer, the Lao, the Thai, the Burmese, and the Javanese, form major ethnic groups and are distributed over a vast geographical area. In addition to paddy farming, these peoples encourage a commodity economy, espouse Buddhism or Islam, possess writing and education systems, and play a central role in the politics, economics, and culture of their countries.

Scattered in the mountainous areas of Southeast Asia are numerous ethnic groups, some of whom subsist by hunting and gathering, although most en-

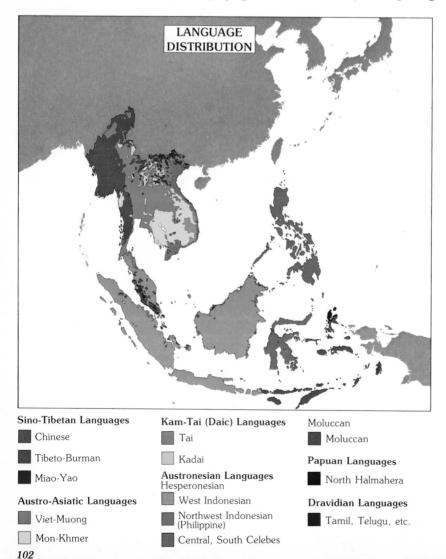

LANGUAGE DISTRIBUTION

Sino-Tibetan Languages
- Chinese
- Tibeto-Burman
- Miao-Yao

Austro-Asiatic Languages
- Viet-Muong
- Mon-Khmer

Kam-Tai (Daic) Languages
- Tai
- Kadai

Austronesian Languages
Hesperonesian
- West Indonesian
- Northwest Indonesian (Philippine)
- Central, South Celebes

Moluccan
- Moluccan

Papuan Languages
- North Halmahera

Dravidian Languages
- Tamil, Telugu, etc.

gage in slash-and-burn agriculture or small-scale paddy farming. These peoples have preserved their indigenous lifestyles by their self-sufficiency and their isolation, and they have their own languages and religions. The second theme of the Southeast Asia exhibit is to show the characteristics of the indigenous lifestyles and cultures of these groups, with displays of costumes, ornaments, weapons, and tools for hunting.

Since ancient times, Southeast Asia, lying between India and China, has been subjected to the cultural influences of these two regions. The influence of Chinese civilization is particularly strong in Vietnam, where Chinese characters were in use until recently and where various other influences are still evident. On the other hand, from around the beginning of the Christian era, southern Indochina and the coastal areas of Sumatra and Java were frequented by Indian merchants, who introduced their political and legal systems and the religions of Brahmanism and Buddhism. Around the first and second centuries, Indianized or Indic

kingdoms were established in mainland Southeast Asia. By the eleventh to thirteenth centuries, powerful kingdoms were founded in Cambodia, central Thailand, Burma (Myanmar), southern Sumatra, and central Java, and elaborate palaces and magnificent temples were built, resulting in the combination of indigenous and Indian cultures. During this period, too, the Thai and the Burmese migrated southward from northern Indochina and eventually founded their own kingdoms. At the same time, Theravada (Hinayana) Buddhism was introduced to mainland Southeast Asia from Sri Lanka, and the thirteenth century saw the spread of Islam, mainly in insular Southeast Asia. In the sixteenth century, with the arrival of the Europeans in Southeast Asia, most parts of this region were colonized, and much of the Philippines, in particular, was Christianized. (Komei Sasaki)

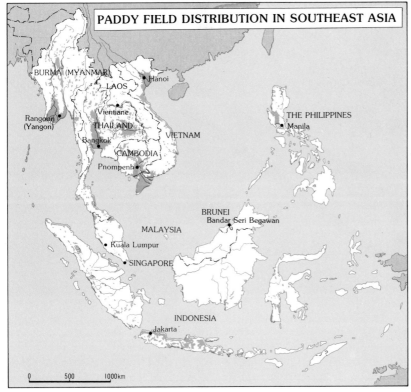

PADDY FIELD DISTRIBUTION IN SOUTHEAST ASIA

In mainland Southeast Asia, paddy fields are concentrated in the deltas of large rivers, and it was here that the kingdoms of Southeast Asia were first established. In insular Southeast Asia, paddy fields are plentiful in Java but sparse on other islands, especially in mountainous regions.

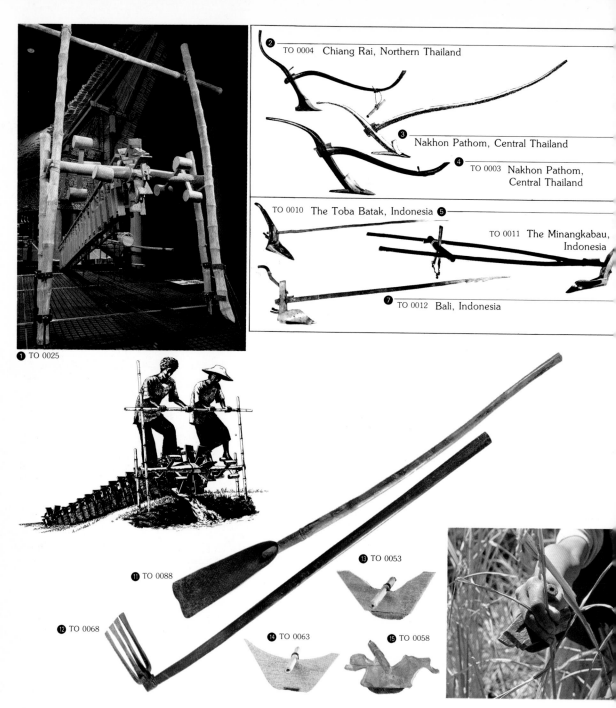

2 TO 0004   Chiang Rai, Northern Thailand

3 Nakhon Pathom, Central Thailand

4 TO 0003   Nakhon Pathom, Central Thailand

TO 0010   The Toba Batak, Indonesia **5**

TO 0011   The Minangkabau, Indonesia

7 TO 0012   Bali, Indonesia

1 TO 0025

11 TO 0088

12 TO 0068

13 TO 0053

14 TO 0063

15 TO 0058

Rice Cultures

In Southeast Asia, many highland ethnic groups engage in slash-and-burn agriculture, but paddy field cultivation dominates the lowlands. This cultivation requires both tilling, for which Chinese- and Indian-type plows are used, and irrigation of large land areas by a variety of methods. Belief in rice spirits is widespread throughout the region, and farmers pray to deities for an abundant harvest. In the harvesting, threshing, and processing of rice, various tools with distinct local characteristics are used, some of which are similar to those found in Japan. Granaries for storing rice panicles or grains, and where rice spirits are believed to reside, are often built on stilts. Rice is usually eaten boiled, but steamed glutinous rice, for which special steamers are used, is also eaten. It is a common dietary habit to eat rice with fish and fermented fish sauces, and freshwater fishing in paddies and rivers employs various tools such as fish traps.

1 **Treadle Wheel** (Nakhon Pathom, Central Thailand) This water wheel, common in the delta regions of mainland Southeast Asia, pumps water up 1 to 1.5 meters from waterways into paddy fields.
2–**10** **Plow Types and Distribution**

TYPES AND DISTRIBUTION OF PLOWS IN SOUTHEAST ASIA (TO 0722)

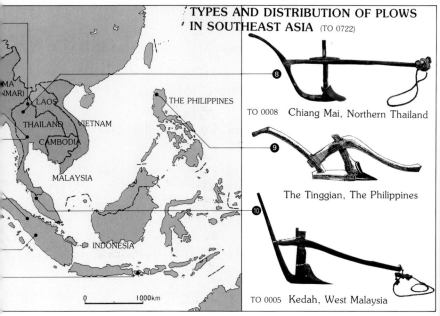

TO 0008 Chiang Mai, Northern Thailand

The Tinggian, The Philippines

TO 0005 Kedah, West Malaysia

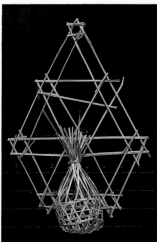

⓴ TO 0215

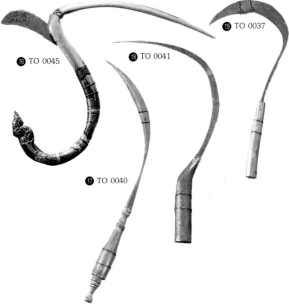

⓭ TO 0045

⓱ TO 0040

⓲ TO 0041

⓳ TO 0037

㉑ TO 0214

㉒ TO 0218

Three types of plows are used in Southeast Asia, and these were influenced by Indian and Chinese plows.

❷–❹ Indian-type Plows
With a short blade at the end of the handle.

❺–❼ Malay-type Plows
Indian in origin, these are found throughout insular Southeast Asia. The short blade can be removed and other blades attached.

❽–❿ Chinese-type Plows
The same type, in which shaft and blade are held in place by a post, is found in Japan.

⓫ Spade (Nakhon Pathom, Central Thailand)
Used to make ridges in paddy fields and remove weeds.

⓬ Hoe (Bali, Indonesia)

In Bali, this is used to prepare paddy fields, which are first hoed and then tilled with a plow.

⓭–⓯ Tools for Harvesting Rice (⓭ West Java, Indonesia; ⓮ Kedah, West Malaysia; ⓯ Palawan, The Philippines)
These tools for cutting rice panicles are mainly used in insular Southeast Asia but are also found in parts of Vietnam, Laos, and Thailand.

⓰–⓳ Sickles (⓰ Battambang, Cambodia; ⓱ Chiang Rai, Northern Thailand; ⓲ Nakhon Pathom, Central Thailand; ⓳ Savannakhet, Laos)
Many sickle blades are toothed, and the degree of blade curvature differs according to location and the height of the rice stalks. Sickles used in delta regions have sharply curved blades to cut stalks that have toppled over.

⓴ Paddy Field Talisman (Ayutthaya, Central Thailand)
Made of bamboo, this talisman is placed in paddy fields to ward off evil spirits.

㉑ Rice Goddess (Ayutthaya, Central Thailand)
Worshiped in harvest rituals. The first panicles of rice, in which the rice goddess is said to reside, are cut ritually.

㉒ Female Rice Spirit (Bali, Indonesia)
Made of palm leaves, this figure is worshiped during agricultural rituals.

① TO 0195·0202·0220, etc.

② TO 0191

③ TO 0190

❶ Threshing
Methods include being stamped on by cattle, being beaten, and the use of a threshing mortar. After threshing, the husks and dust are blown away when the rice is thrown into the air with a winnowing basket or by using fans. A variety of implements are involved in the process.

⑤ TO 0262

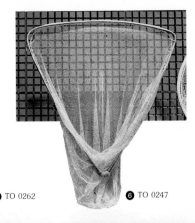

⑥ TO 0247

⑦ TO 0270

④ TO 0226, etc.

⑧ TO 0276 (left) · 0277

⑨ TO 0271–0275 · 0797 · 0798

❷ Large Threshing Basket (Chiang Rai, Northern Thailand)
Bundles of cut rice stalks are beaten against the inside of this basket of woven bamboo.

❸ Ox Cart (Chiang Mai, Northern Thailand)
An important means of transportation and conveyance in all Southeast Asian lowlands.

❹ Fish Traps (*extreme left*: Battambang, Cambodia)
These traps are usually made of bamboo and placed in rivers, canals, and swamps. Their shapes and sizes differ according to the kind of fish to be caught and where the traps are placed.

❺ Fishing Basket (Nakhon Pathom, Central Thailand)
Common throughout Southeast Asia, this basket is placed over freshwater fish in the water, and the fish are caught by inserting the hand into the basket from the top.

❻ Fishing Net (Nakhon Pathom, Central Thailand)
Freshwater fishing and rice cultivation go hand in hand. This net is used to scoop up fish in paddy fields and rivers.

❼ Four-armed Net (West Java, Indonesia)
Used to catch small river fish, which are sometimes then raised in paddy fields.

❽ Boats (*left*: The Toba Batak, Indonesia; *right*: Nakhon Pathom, Central Thailand)
The boat on the left is used for fishing on Lake Toba, and the other is used for transportation and in harvesting rice.

❾ Paddles (Sarawak, East Malaysia; the Senoi, West Malaysia, etc.)
Short paddles are used in the sitting position. Oars with pointed tips are used in swamps.

107

1 TO 0436

2 TO 0201

3 TO 0483

5 TO 0442
TO 0437

4 TO 0432

6 TO 0397

7 TO 0477

1 Stone Grinder (Bangkok, Central Thailand)
Although grains are usually consumed whole in areas where rice is cultivated, sometimes they are ground into flour. This stone mill is used for grinding grains and beans into flour.

2 Threshing and Hulling Tool (Central Java, Indonesia)
This tool can also be used for grinding and pounding, as well as for polishing rice.

3 Glutinous Rice Steamer (Chiang Mai, Northern Thailand)
Peoples in Laos, northern Thailand, and southwestern China—the areas of glutinous rice cultivation—eat steamed glutinous rice as the staple food.

4 Food Container (Sumba, Indonesia)
This type of lidded container for cooked rice or dried fish is found throughout Southeast Asia.

5 Spice Mortar (The Toba Batak, Indonesia)
Used to crush and mix spices, such as black pepper and chili.

6 Lacquered Spoon (South Sumatra, Indonesia)
Lacquer techniques originated in mainland areas and were adopted in Palembang, Indonesia.

7 Coconut Milk Strainer (Bangkok, Central Thailand)
Used when grated coconut is kneaded with water to make coconut milk.

8 Coconut Graters (*from top*: Mindanao, The Philippines; Bali, Indonesia; West Java, Indonesia)
These are for grating copra to make coconut milk, used in cooking from India to Oceania.

8 TO 0475・0473・0474 (from top)

The Lifestyle of Mountain Peoples

Many ethnic groups are found in mountainous areas in both mainland and insular Southeast Asia. The languages spoken by them belong to several families, including Sino-Tibetan and Austronesian. Hamlets of about twenty to thirty households are common on mountain ridges and slopes, and the houses have earthen floors, raised floors, or a combination of both. The main means of livelihood is slash-and-burn agriculture, although many men also engage in hunting. In slash-and-burn agriculture, upland rice, maize, and millets such as sorghum and foxtail millet are cultivated. Unlike paddies, fields must be left fallow for long periods because of soil deterioration. Therefore, groups such as the Yao and the Miao frequently move around and are spread over a wide area from southern China to northern Southeast Asia. A striking characteristic of mountain groups is the colorful costumes, especially of the women, who wear a variety of personal ornaments with traditional designs that also serve as a means of identifying the ethnic groups.

❾ Man's and Woman's Clothing (The Lisu, Northern Thailand)
The colorful patchwork on the sleeves of the woman's blouse and the turban decorated with beads over the front brim are characteristic of the Lisu.
❿ Woman's Clothing (The Hmong [Miao], Northern Thailand)
Clothing of the group called the Blue Hmong. Pleated batik skirts are distinctively Hmong.
⓫ Man's and Woman's Clothing (The Yao, Northern Thailand)
The embroidery of flowers (symbolizing a blue dragon and a white tiger) on the woman's turban and trousers is peculiar to the Yao.

❿ TO 0280

❾ TO 0282

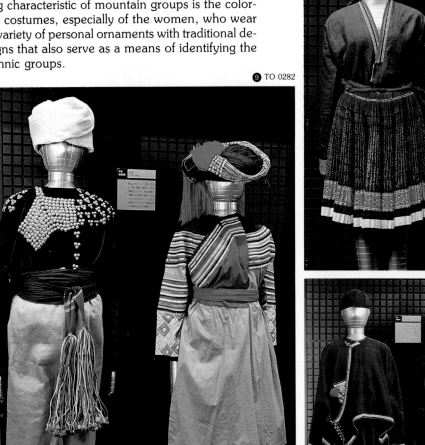

⓫ TO 0281

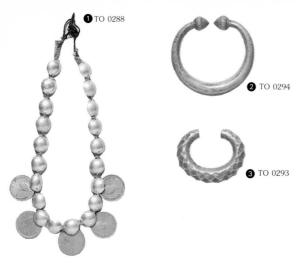

❶ TO 0288

❷ TO 0294

❸ TO 0293

❶ **Necklace** (The Akha, Northern Thailand)
A necklace commonly worn by Akha women. Indian silver coins dating to that country's colonial period are especially valued by women.
❷–❸ **Bracelets** (The Hmong, Northern Thailand)
These ornaments are used by both men and women. Some silver bracelets are used as charms to ward off evil spirits.

Gatherer-Hunters and Boat Dwellers

Peoples who gather plants and hunt small animals form small groups dispersed in the mountain regions of Southeast Asia, and these groups trade with the farmers in adjacent areas. Along the coasts of the Malay Peninsula, Indonesia, and the southern Philippines, boat dwellers engage in small-scale sea trading, fishing, and the gathering of plants. Although both types of groups used to live by moving around in their territories, they are now becoming sedentary farmers or fishermen.

❹ TO 0589–0604

❺ TO 0625–0628

❽ TO 0970

❾ TO 0618

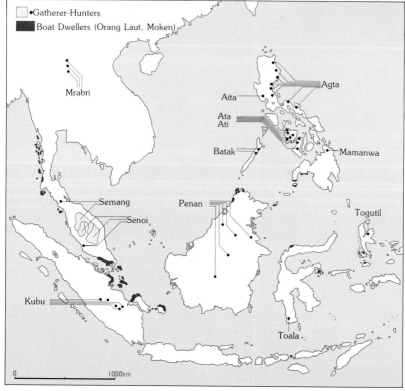

❹ Arrows (Mindanao, The Philippines)

Used by mountain peoples for hunting small animals such as monkeys and fowl. The bamboo tips are dressed with poison.

❺–❼ Blowpipes and Darts

These blowpipes, darts, and quivers are used for hunting by the mountain peoples of insular Southeast Asia, including West Malaysia. A piece of cork is attached to the end of each dart so it fits into the blowpipe, and the tips are dressed with poison.

❽–❿ Shields

Made of wood, bark, or leather and originally for protection in battle, shields are now used by some ethnic groups only in dances.

⓯–⓲ Swords (⓯–⓰ Sarawak, East Malaysia; ⓱–⓲ The Philippines)

Carried by the men of the mountain peoples at their waists as weapons, such swords with decorated hilts and sheaths are also used as farming implements.

⓳–㉒ Spears

Used by the mountain peoples of insular Southeast Asia as weapons, for hunting, and for various ceremonies, such as war dances.

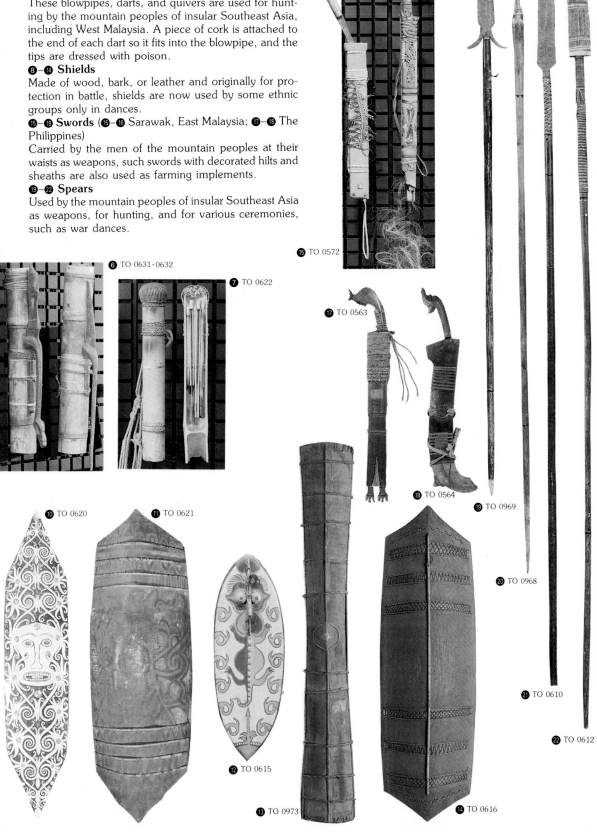

❻ TO 0631·0632

❼ TO 0622

⓰ TO 0570

⓯ TO 0572

⓱ TO 0563

⓲ TO 0564

⓳ TO 0969

❿ TO 0620

⓫ TO 0621

⓴ TO 0968

㉑ TO 0610

㉒ TO 0612

⓬ TO 0615

⓭ TO 0973

⓮ TO 0616

❶ TO 0527・0954, etc.

❷ TO 0137, etc.

❶ **Hats**
Both lowlanders and mountain peoples wear hats of various shapes, designs, and colors to keep off the sun, rather than the rain.

❷ **Back Baskets**
Of rattan, bamboo, bark, or vine, these are made and used mainly by the mountain peoples.

Religious Life

Buddhism, particularly Theravada (Hinayana) Buddhism, is widespread in mainland Southeast Asia and has a profound influence on people's lives. Islam has taken root in Malaysia, Indonesia, and the southern Philippines, and Christianity (primarily Catholicism) has permeated most other parts of the Philippines. Animism also exists in Southeast Asia, transmitted by peoples in mountainous areas and outlying islands. The animistic tradition was syncretized with imported religions such as Buddhism, and thrives in the religious life of people in both cities and rural communities.

❸ **Spirit Shrine** (replica) (Bangkok, Central Thailand) Many Thais set up such small shrines in yards for the land spirit that protects the house and yard, and daily offerings and prayers are made for the safety and health of the residents.

❹ **Sutra Box** (replica) (Chiang Mai, Northern Thailand) In the temples of northern Thailand, sutras are kept in elaborately decorated lacquered boxes.

❺ **Thai Buddhism**
On the raised dais at left is a Buddhist altar, with, below it, ceremonial paraphernalia used when a person enters the Buddhist monkhood, which is encouraged at least once in every man's life. At right is a chair from which sermons are given in temples during important Buddhist rituals.

❸ TO 0980

❹ TO 0682

❺ TO 0674, etc.

❶ Phra Malai Sutra (Bangkok, Central Thailand)
The Phra Malai Sutra explains the teachings of Buddhism to the people in a simplified manner. It is written in the Khmer script and was used in Thailand in the nineteenth century. Phra Malai was a Sri Lankan monk who had supernatural powers and visited heaven and hell.

❷ Bronze Drum (Laos)
The date and place of origin of this drum are unknown, but such bronze drums are believed to be ceremonial instruments of the bronze culture of Southeast Asia and China. Though used mainly in northern Indochina, they are found throughout the region bounded by the Yangzi River in the north and Indonesia in the south.

❸ Grave Figure (The Toraja, Indonesia)
Several types of graves are found among the Sa'dan Toraja people: specially hollowed-out caves in mountainsides for the ruling class, and natural caves or rock crevices for the common people. An image of the dead person is placed before the grave in his or her honor.

❶ TO 0681

❸ TO 0919

❷ TO 0637

❹ TO 0666

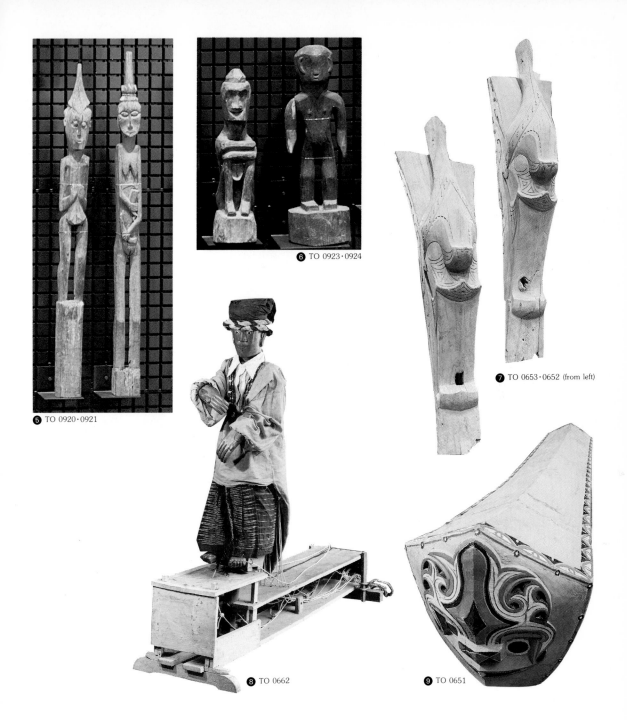

❺ TO 0920·0921

❻ TO 0923·0924

❼ TO 0653·0652 (from left)

❽ TO 0662

❾ TO 0651

❹ **Large Drum** (Chiang Mai, Northern Thailand)
A temple drum used in important ceremonies, such as a novice ordination in northern Thailand. In the evening prior to such ceremonies, young men vie with one another in beating the drum.

❺ **Ancestral Figures** (The Dayak, Indonesia)
These wooden figures, made by the mountain people of Borneo, are set up close to the house to ward off evil spirits believed to bring illness and other misfortunes.

❻ **Spirit Figures** (The Ifugao, The Philippines)
Wooden figures made by the Ifugao, a mountain people of northern Luzon, are usually enshrined in granaries. In ceremonies connected with agriculture or healing, priests use the figures to invoke ancestral and other spirits, which then take up residence in the figures.

❼ **Beam Ornaments** (The Toba Batak, Indonesia)
In northern Sumatra, ornaments resembling human faces are affixed to the ends of beams projecting in front of granaries. They are said to represent deities of the Toba Batak religion, which was strongly influenced by Indian culture.

❽ **Dancing Doll** (The Toba Batak, Indonesia)
If a man dies childless, a doll in his image is made to dance as if it were alive at the funeral in order to prevent the spirits of his ancestors from wandering into this world and bringing misfortune.

❾ **Coffin** (The Toba Batak, Indonesia)
Made of the trunk of a jackfruit tree, with a carving resembling a face on the front to represent a deity.

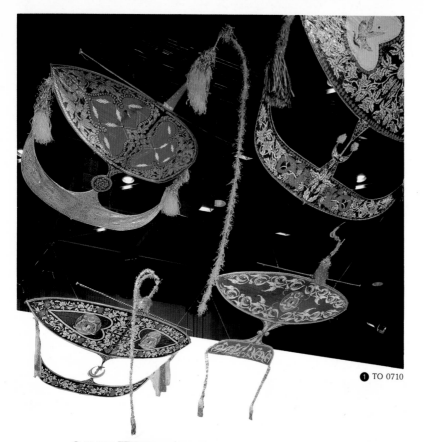

❶ TO 0710

❷ TO 0889

❸ TO 0888

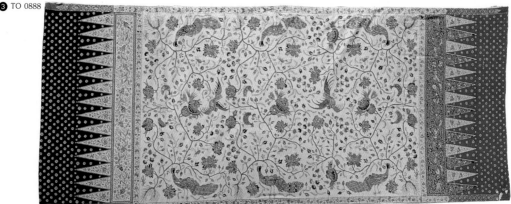

Arts and Crafts

The ethnic groups of Southeast Asia have fine crafts, including metalwork, woodwork, lacquerware, dyeing, weaving, ceramics, and earthenware. Some of these crafts have been fostered by indigenous cultures, while others reflect the influence of the Chinese, Indian, and European civilizations and Islamic culture. Many are simple, but some employ highly refined techniques. Ikat (textiles woven with tie-dyed thread) and batik (textiles with wax-resist dyeing) are known throughout the world. Southeast Asia is also rich in the performing arts, in which the people take great pleasure. Many Southeast Asian arts have religious and ritual elements, through which communication is made with deities and spirits. Such arts are thus often performed during ceremonies to worship deities and spirits, including ancestral spirits, and during rites of passage celebrating birth, puberty, marriage, and death.

❶ **Kites** (Kelantan, West Malaysia)
The kite-flying contest held after the rice harvest has a religious basis of welcoming the spirits of the wind and the sky.
❷ **Tubular Sarong** (Roti, Indonesia)
A woman's tubular sarong of typical Indonesian warp ikat with floral and striped patterns.
❸ **Wrap-around Sarong** (South Sulawesi, Indonesia)
A wrap-around sarong of cotton batik made in Java.
❹ **Wrap-around Sarong** (Bali, Indonesia)
A man's ceremonial wrap-around sarong with geometrical patterns woven with weft ikat and supplementary weft techniques.

❺ TO 0909·0910

❹ TO 0979

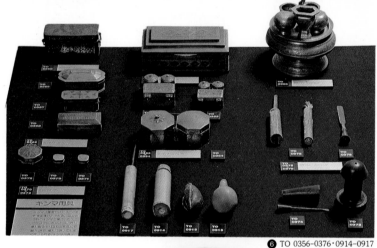

❻ TO 0356-0376·0914-0917

❼ TO 0382-0396

❺ **Looms** (*left*: The Toba Batak, Indonesia; *right*: The Ifugao, The Philippines)
A back-tension loom with its continuous looped warp threads is the oldest type used in Southeast Asia.
❻-❼ **Accessories for Betel-chewing** (❻ The Philippines, Malaysia, Indonesia; ❼ Thailand)
Widespread in Southeast Asia is the custom of betel-

chewing, in which materials such as betel nut, lime, gambier, and tobacco are wrapped in a betel leaf and chewed. Scissors to cut betel nuts and gambier, tools to crush and mix the lime and betel nut, and the containers for these materials have delicate decoration done with various techniques.

1 TO 0689

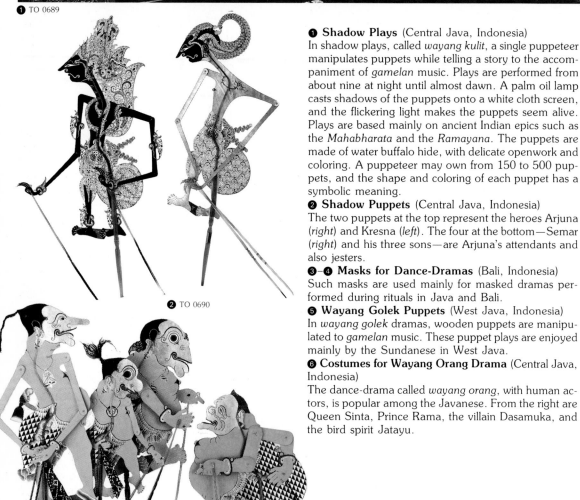

2 TO 0690

❶ Shadow Plays (Central Java, Indonesia)
In shadow plays, called *wayang kulit*, a single puppeteer manipulates puppets while telling a story to the accompaniment of *gamelan* music. Plays are performed from about nine at night until almost dawn. A palm oil lamp casts shadows of the puppets onto a white cloth screen, and the flickering light makes the puppets seem alive. Plays are based mainly on ancient Indian epics such as the *Mahabharata* and the *Ramayana*. The puppets are made of water buffalo hide, with delicate openwork and coloring. A puppeteer may own from 150 to 500 puppets, and the shape and coloring of each puppet has a symbolic meaning.

❷ Shadow Puppets (Central Java, Indonesia)
The two puppets at the top represent the heroes Arjuna (*right*) and Kresna (*left*). The four at the bottom—Semar (*right*) and his three sons—are Arjuna's attendants and also jesters.

❸–❹ Masks for Dance-Dramas (Bali, Indonesia)
Such masks are used mainly for masked dramas performed during rituals in Java and Bali.

❺ Wayang Golek Puppets (West Java, Indonesia)
In *wayang golek* dramas, wooden puppets are manipulated to *gamelan* music. These puppet plays are enjoyed mainly by the Sundanese in West Java.

❻ Costumes for Wayang Orang Drama (Central Java, Indonesia)
The dance-drama called *wayang orang*, with human actors, is popular among the Javanese. From the right are Queen Sinta, Prince Rama, the villain Dasamuka, and the bird spirit Jatayu.

⑤ TO 0709

③ TO 0819

④ TO 0822

⑥ TO 0696–0699

❶–❷ Barong and Rangda (Bali, Indonesia)
The *Barong* dance, which portrays a life-and-death struggle between these two figures, is performed in a ritual to banish evil spirits. It is based on a view of the world as a struggle between the forces of good and evil. Barong is a mystical, sacred beast symbolizing good and light, and two men perform the dance inside the costume. Rangda, who fights with Barong, is a female demon symbolizing evil and darkness.
❸ Dance Horse (Central Java, Indonesia)
In dances such as the *jatilan*, a man who is possessed by spirits imitates a horse. Many Javanese dances originated at court, but this is a rare folk dance, which was originally a religious dance to ward off the plague. Though it was formerly performed by farmers, it is now performed in marketplaces and at roadsides by wandering artists.

❶ TO 0702

❷ TO 0701

❸ TO 0707

The Cultures of Central and North Asia

Central and North Asia denotes the area of the Asian continent east of a line drawn from the east coast of the Caspian Sea to the Ural Mountains and including Mongolia and Siberia. Since ancient times, stock farming in the steppes, agriculture in oases areas and in foothills, and trade in the cities have been pursued in this region, which has witnessed cultural exchange from all directions. The ethnic groups show great variety in composition, as well as in clothing, food, and forms of shelter. Central and North Asia constitute a continuous landmass, and consequently share deep ethnic and cultural links.

The term "Central Asia" is used to denote three slightly different areas. The first, also known as Western Turkistan, is the region circumscribed by the Siberian grasslands to the north, by the borders of the Soviet Union, Iran, and Afghanistan to the south, by the Caspian Sea to the west, and by the Pamir Range and the Tian Shan Mountains to the east. The second area comprises Western Turkistan and Eastern Turkistan, now China's Xinjiang Uighur Autonomous Region. The third area denotes the largest region, which includes the Sayan Mountains, the Altai Mountains, and the Mongolian Plateau or highlands, the Takla Makan Desert, and the Tibetan Plateau, as well as Western Turkistan. This exhibit assumes the first description, and so Central Asia is considered to consist of the five Soviet republics of Kazakh, Uzbek, Kirgiz, Turkmen, and Tadzhik. Although Iranian languages are spoken in Tadzhik, most of the peoples in the other parts of the region speak Turkic languages.

Nomadic peoples, known as the Saka (Scythians), were active on the plains, or steppes, as early as the year 1000 B.C. and were closely related to the agricultural people of the oasis regions in the south. Most steppe inhabitants spoke Iranian languages until about the beginning of the Middle Ages, but after that the use of Turkic languages spread. The Sogd Iranian people, however, left a cultural legacy throughout Central Asia as a result of their trade along the Silk Road. After the seventh century, Islam spread across Central Asia.

In addition to the peoples already mentioned, Slavs (Russians, Ukrainians, and Belorussians), Kara-Kalpaks, Uighurs, Dungans, Koreans, Jewish Central Asians, Gypsies, and Arabs also reside in contemporary Central Asia. The interfacing of agricultural life in the oases and nomadic life in the steppes is explored in the "Agricultural and Nomadic Cultures" display.

North Asia is made up of the Mongolian Plateau and Siberia. Southern Siberia and Mongolia are steppe regions, and to the north of them lies the vast taiga, or forest belt, extending as far as the tundra region of permafrost that skirts the Arctic Ocean. The Mongolian Plateau, now the Mongolian People's Republic, consists of grasslands with an average altitude of 1,600 meters, and they were formerly the home of nomads. The native people—the Buryat, Torgut, Olyot, Zakhchin, Bait,

Derbet, and Khalkha peoples—all speak Mongolian languages, with the Khalkha constituting about 75 percent of the entire population. In the northwest, the Khoton, Tuvan, and Kazakh peoples speak Turkic languages.

Nomadic domestication of animals came to dominate the grasslands of Mongolia around the tenth century B.C. Feudalism was established in the thirteenth century, after the rule of Genghis Khan, and continued for seven centuries until the socialist revolution of 1921. Tibetan Buddhism, or Lamaism, became the dominant religion in Mongolia from about the latter half of the sixteenth century. All these had a considerable influence on the traditional cultures of Mongolia. In the Mongolian People's Republic today, agriculture, the mining of minerals, and industrialization are developing alongside stock farming. "The Nomadic Cultures of Mongolia" exhibit focuses on traditional North Asian nomadic culture.

Siberia is roughly 4,000 kilometers east to west and 2,000 kilometers north to south. Some of the major rivers of the world, such as the Amur, Lena, Yenisey, and Ob, flow through it, and in adddition there are countless lakes and marshes. Living in harmony with their natural environment, the people of northern Siberia hunt, fish, and raise reindeer, while in the south they engage in agriculture and stock farming.

In linguistic terms, the Khant and Mansi peoples who inhabit the western lowlands of Siberia belong to the Finno-Ugrian family, and the Nenets and Sel'kup belong to the Samoyedic family. In southern Siberia and the Yakut Autonomous Soviet Socialist Republic are found the Yakut, Khakas, Altay, Tuvan, and Shor peoples, who speak Turkic languages. The Buryat in the Buryat Autonomous Soviet Socialist Republic and in southeastern Siberia speak Mongolian languages. The Orochi, Ul'chi, Nanay, Even, and Evenki peoples, who live in the vast region stretching from the Yenisey River to Sakhalin Island belong to the Tungus language group. The Koryak and Chukchi, living in northeastern Siberia, the Nivkhi (Gilyak) in northern Sakhalin and the lower reaches of the Amur River, and the Ket in the middle reaches of the Yenisey River have their own distinctive languages termed Paleo-Asiatic.

Rituals associated with hunting and fishing developed among the peoples of North Asia, and an important role is played by shamanism, which centered on the belief that shamans can communicate directly with spirits, can heal sickness, and can predict the future. Yet this tradition, too, is fast disappearing. "The World of Shamanism" display presents the spiritual world of the Siberian people, and "The Cultures of Hunting and Fishing Peoples" re-creates the lifestyles of people in the harsh environments of North Asia. (Kyuzo Kato)

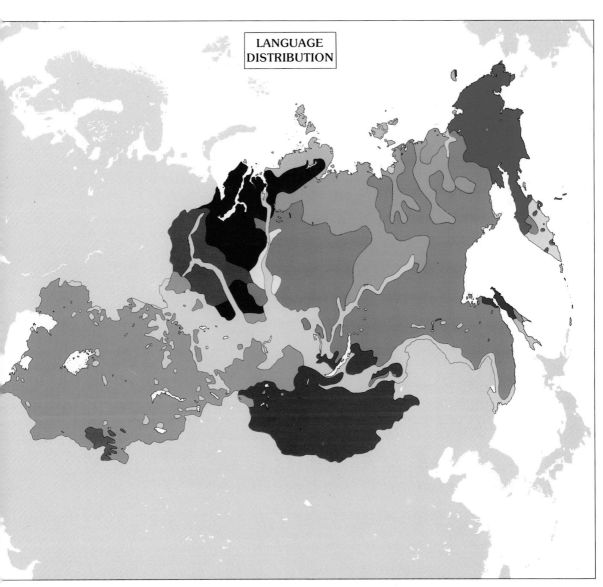

LANGUAGE DISTRIBUTION

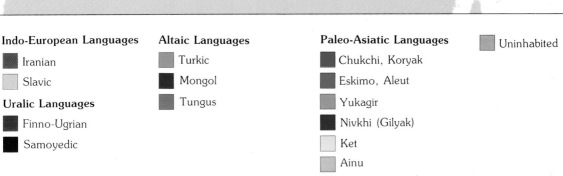

Indo-European Languages
- Iranian
- Slavic

Uralic Languages
- Finno-Ugrian
- Samoyedic

Altaic Languages
- Turkic
- Mongol
- Tungus

Paleo-Asiatic Languages
- Chukchi, Koryak
- Eskimo, Aleut
- Yukagir
- Nivkhi (Gilyak)
- Ket
- Ainu

- Uninhabited

❷ TK 0006

❸ TK 0005

❹ TK 0011

Agricultural and Nomadic Cultures

Since ancient times Central Asia has been a region of contact between oasis farmers of the southern steppes and the nomads of the northern steppes. At the same time, it has served as a route of communication between China in the east and the Mediterranean in the west. The natural environment of Central Asia is mainly treeless grassland, semidesert, or desert, with some mountains and river oases. The occupations of the people between the eighteenth and the early twentieth centuries were: permanent farming in the oases, using plows and irrigation; stock (mainly horses and camels) farming in the steppes, with the animals turned loose on the grasslands all year round; and semipermanent (half stock farming , half crop farming) on the land in between. Occasionally, fishing was also combined with one of these occupations. Agriculture was of three types: irrigated farming on flat land, supported by the cooperative construction of irrigation canals; small-scale irrigated farming utilizing streams in mountain areas; and farming by natural irrigation, which was limited to areas where the spring rainfall was plentiful. Some nomadic groups regularly traversed the grasslands from east to west or north to south, while others moved north and south to and from the mountains.

❶ Bridal Costumes and Traditional Clothing (*from left*: The Uzbek, Tadzhik, Turkmen, Kirgiz, and Turkmen)

All these are made of wool. The white bridal costumes are decorated with beaded tassels and silver thread.

❷ Dress (The Uzbek, Central Asia)

Of cotton and decorated with silk thread, this typical Uzbek woman's dress is worn over trousers.

❸ Dress (The Tadzhik, Central Asia)

Made of cotton and silk for a young married woman, the hem, sleeves, and front are decorated with colorful embroidery.

❹ Woman's Vest (The Kirgiz, Central Asia)

With green and yellow embroidery on red velvet.

❺ Man's Outer Garment (The Kirgiz, Central Asia)

With red and blue embroidery on black velvet.

❻ Woman's Coat (The Kazakh, Central Asia)

A velvet coat decorated with embroidery.

❼–❽ Socks (The Turkmen and Tadzhik, Central Asia)

Woolen socks are well suited to arid regions with drastic temperature changes.

❾ Caps

The shape, color, and pattern of a cap indicate the gender, ethnic group, and the place of origin of the wearer.

❿ Uzbek Accessories

The necklaces and bridal coronet are of silver. Brown semiprecious stones are symbols of good fortune to the Turkic peoples.

⓫ Turkmen Accessories

Central Asian women wear silver accessories on their foreheads, ears, and chests. Brown semiprecious stones are prized from Central Asia to West Asia.

❾ TK 0031, etc.

❺ TK 0008

❿ TK 0083–0087

❼ TK 0603

⓫ TK 0059–
TK 0070

❽ TK 0601

❻ TK 0012

❹ TK 0577

❷ TK 0101

❸ TK 0459–0509

❶ **Cart, Horse Saddles, Bridle, and Whip** (The Uzbek, Central Asia)
This cart, to be pulled by a horse, has large wheels to make it easy to ford streams. The saddles are leather-covered wooden frames.

❷ **Tapestry** (The Uzbek, Central Asia)
With silk embroidery on velvet. Embroidery with gold thread flourished in the old capital of Bukhara, where craftsmen were patronized by the court.

❸ **Clay Whistles** (The Tadzhik, Central Asia)
These toys of painted baked clay have fanciful shapes representing legendary creatures.

❹ **Jar** (The Uzbek, Central Asia)
This jar is basically unglazed, although there are traces of glaze around the mouth.

❺ **Pitcher** (The Uzbek, Central Asia)
Made of beaten brass, such pitchers with pleasing curves are seen throughout Central Asia.

❻ **Container** (The Uzbek, Central Asia)
Of beaten brass with patterns on the outer surface.

❼ **Ladle and Pot** (The Uzbek, Central Asia)
Water is boiled in this beaten brass pot, then tea leaves are added and steeped. Green tea is preferred in Central Asia.

❽ **Tashkent Dwelling** (1/10 scale model) (The Uzbek, Central Asia)
This is modeled on the home of a middle-class merchant built about a century ago.

❾ **Kitchen** (scale model) (The Uzbek, Central Asia)
The oven at the far end of the room is for baking *non*, a kind of bread. Heat from the fire underneath passes up through the walls of the oven, and the dough is stuck onto the interior walls with gloved hands or a type of shovel.

❿ **Woman's Room from Samarkand** (model) (The Uzbek, Central Asia)
Women's rooms are set apart from rooms for men and guests, and guests are generally not permitted to see a woman's face.

❺ TK 0593

❾ TK 0671

❻ TK 0587

❼ TK 0584・0590

❿ TK 0672

● TK 0090

❷ TK 0103

❸ TK 0095

❶ **Carpet** (The Turkmen, Central Asia)
Rug-making is a typical Turkmen craft, with patterns vary-ing according to the ethnic group.
❷ **Pouch** (The Kirgiz, Central Asia)
This pouch, made by sewing brightly colored pieces of

felt together, was for keeping personal articles in.
❸ **Embroidered Wall-hanging** (The Kazakh, Central Asia)
Nomads used to brighten their tents by placing long, colorfully embroidered strips of cloth across the ceiling.

The Nomadic Cultures of Mongolia

Nomadism is a form of stock farming. Although there are different degrees of nomadism, nomadism and seminomadism now occur in no less than thirty countries around the world. Among these, Mongolia has the longest history of nomadism. Just as Asia's agricultural peoples speak of the "five grains" (rice, barley, millet, beans, and foxtail millet), so the Mongolians refer to five domesticated animals: the horse, sheep, goat, cow, and camel. With the exception of the Gobi Desert in the south and southeast, Mongolia is a land of lush pastures ideal for grazing, which gave rise to nomadic stock farming, the traditional means of livelihood there. From their animals, the nomads obtain valuable leather, milk, and meat. However, the standard of living of the Mongolian peoples was held in check by the feudal system that began in the early thirteenth century, by two centuries of Chinese Qing-dynasty rule, and by four hundred years of Lamaist rule. The Mongolian people were greatly affected by the socialist revolution of 1921, and their nomadic lifestyle is now shifting toward one centering on agriculture, industry, and mining.

❹ Mongolian Clothing
Traditional Khalkha women's clothing consists of a vest (*uji*) worn over a one-piece dress (*ternob*).
❺ Hats (Mongolia)
Hats made of felt, cloth, and fur for Khalkha men and children, and for Buryat men and women.
❻ Mongolian Yurt
Produced in a factory near Ulan Bator, the furniture is modern but bears traditional patterns.

❹ TK 0604–0608

❺ TK 0149–0161

❻ TK 0121

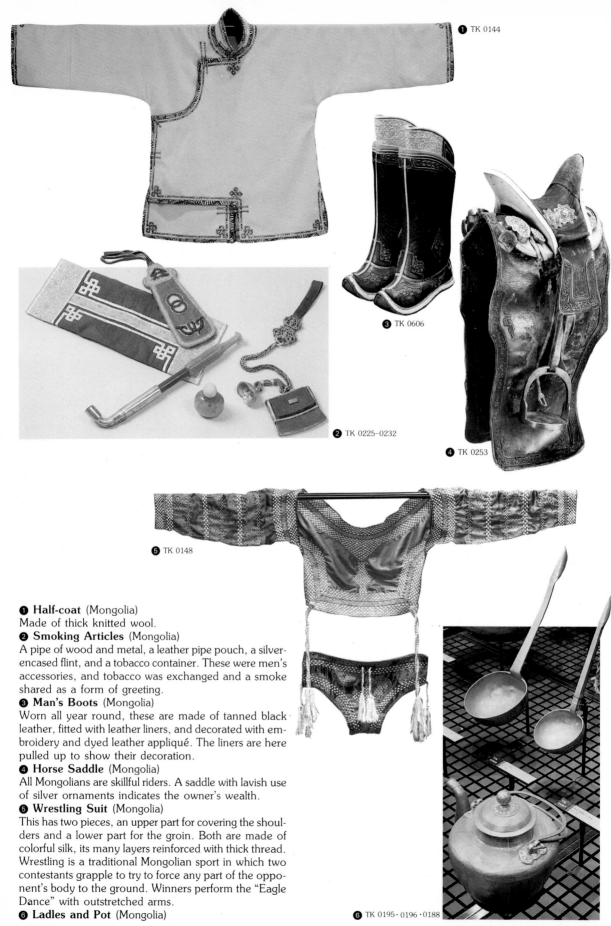

❶ TK 0144

❸ TK 0606

❹ TK 0253

❷ TK 0225–0232

❺ TK 0148

❶ **Half-coat** (Mongolia)
Made of thick knitted wool.

❷ **Smoking Articles** (Mongolia)
A pipe of wood and metal, a leather pipe pouch, a silver-encased flint, and a tobacco container. These were men's accessories, and tobacco was exchanged and a smoke shared as a form of greeting.

❸ **Man's Boots** (Mongolia)
Worn all year round, these are made of tanned black leather, fitted with leather liners, and decorated with embroidery and dyed leather appliqué. The liners are here pulled up to show their decoration.

❹ **Horse Saddle** (Mongolia)
All Mongolians are skillful riders. A saddle with lavish use of silver ornaments indicates the owner's wealth.

❺ **Wrestling Suit** (Mongolia)
This has two pieces, an upper part for covering the shoulders and a lower part for the groin. Both are made of colorful silk, its many layers reinforced with thick thread. Wrestling is a traditional Mongolian sport in which two contestants grapple to try to force any part of the opponent's body to the ground. Winners perform the "Eagle Dance" with outstretched arms.

❻ **Ladles and Pot** (Mongolia)

❻ TK 0195・0196・0188

130

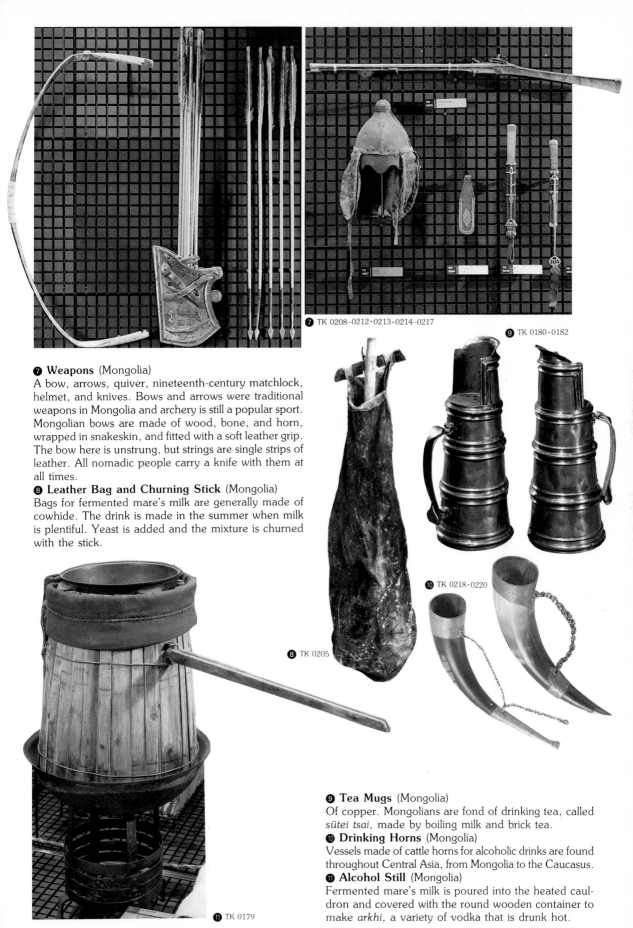

7 Weapons (Mongolia)

A bow, arrows, quiver, nineteenth-century matchlock, helmet, and knives. Bows and arrows were traditional weapons in Mongolia and archery is still a popular sport. Mongolian bows are made of wood, bone, and horn, wrapped in snakeskin, and fitted with a soft leather grip. The bow here is unstrung, but strings are single strips of leather. All nomadic people carry a knife with them at all times.

8 Leather Bag and Churning Stick (Mongolia)

Bags for fermented mare's milk are generally made of cowhide. The drink is made in the summer when milk is plentiful. Yeast is added and the mixture is churned with the stick.

7 TK 0208–0212·0213·0214–0217

9 TK 0180·182

10 TK 0218·0220

8 TK 0205

11 TK 0179

9 Tea Mugs (Mongolia)

Of copper. Mongolians are fond of drinking tea, called *sütei tsai*, made by boiling milk and brick tea.

10 Drinking Horns (Mongolia)

Vessels made of cattle horns for alcoholic drinks are found throughout Central Asia, from Mongolia to the Caucasus.

11 Alcohol Still (Mongolia)

Fermented mare's milk is poured into the heated cauldron and covered with the round wooden container to make *arkhi*, a variety of vodka that is drunk hot.

1 TK 0635·0632

2 TK 0610

3 TK 0244

4 TK 0612
TK 0613
TK 0614

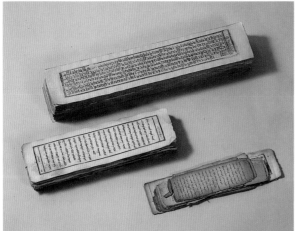

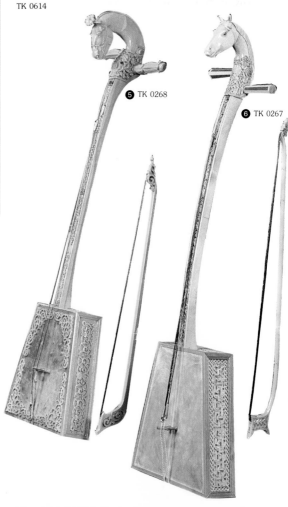

5 TK 0268

6 TK 0267

1 Stone Figures (The Tuvan, Siberia)
Goats, sheep, lions, and horses made of stone or reindeer bone function as amulets.

2 Tsam Mask (Mongolia)
Tsam is a dance at Lamaist temple ceremonies in which masks of deities, animals, and demons are used.

3 Buddhist Image (Mongolia)
Protective deities called "Dharmapālas" are often portrayed in Mongolian Buddhist pictures battling the enemies of Lamaism, and are usually depicted with angry expressions.

4 Sutras (Mongolia)
Formerly nearly one-third of the male population of Mongolia were said to be lamas. The Perfection of Wisdom in Eight Thousand Lines Sutra, shown at the top, was printed in Mongolia.

5–6 Horse-headed Lutes (Mongolia)
With a square body, a goatskin belly, a long fingerboard decorated at the end with a horse's head, and strings and bow made of horsetail hair.

The World of Shamanism

According to indigenous Siberian peoples, human beings are given life by benign and malevolent deities. The former bestow all good things, including food such as fish and animals. Every living plant or animal has a spirit, and all are controlled by deities. Since even benign deities will only listen to human beings when they petition with a pure heart, people make sacrificial offerings. Malevolent deities, on the other hand, are always seeking ways of bringing misfortune to mankind, including death, sickness, and a myriad natural disasters. The original shamans were individuals who had the power to fight or negotiate with such deities or to avoid calamities.

❼–❾ Ceremonial Headdresses (Sakhalin)
Made of wood shavings bound together, these headdresses worn by Uilta (Orok) and Nivkhi (Gilyak) men for various rituals are similar to those made by the neighboring Ainu, but are distinguished by the shavings hanging down at the back.

❿–⓫ Sacred Images (Sakhalin)
The Nivkhi (Gilyak) and the Uilta (Orok) worship wooden images in the form of animals and human beings.

⓬ Shaman Costumes (*from left*: The Yakut, Siberia; the Tuvan, Siberia and Sakhalin)
When conducting rites, shamans don a headdress and special heavy garments with bells and metal fittings sewn on them. The Yakut ordinarily use cow or reindeer leather, and the tassels and metal fittings on the front and back all have magical powers.

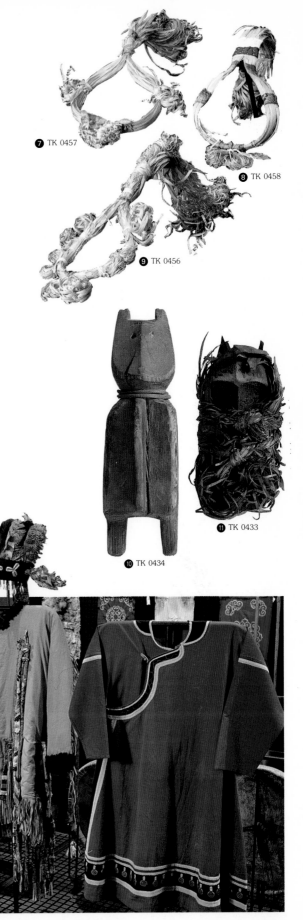

❼ TK 0457

❽ TK 0458

❾ TK 0456

⓫ TK 0433

❿ TK 0434

⓬ TK 0318
TK 0660
TK 0456

① TK 0460 **②** TK 0459
TK 0661

③ TK 0327–0382

④ TK 0465

①–② **Large Shaman Drums** (*from left*: The Uilta, Sakhalin; the Tuvan, Siberia)
In their rituals, North Asian shamans always use wooden drums covered with skin, skillfully made to produce different tones.

③ **Images of Spirits** (replicas) (Siberia)
The names and roles of images of sacred spirits vary somewhat according to ethnic group and location. The life-size image in the center, for example, is from the Udehey. The abdominal portion is hollowed out to show that the spirit is always hungry and ready to eat any evil spirit that approaches.

④ **Belt** (Sakhalin)
Worn around the waist in shamanistic rites. The metal rings of various sizes on the belt are believed to possess spiritual power.

The Cultures of Hunting and Fishing Peoples

The indigenous peoples of Siberia are made up of almost thirty small groups. They are classified linguistically as speakers of Turkic, Mongolian, Tungus, Samoyedic, and Finno-Ugrian languages, and there are also languages that are unrelated to any of those, such as Chukchi, Koryak, Itel'men, Yukagir, and Nivkhi (Gilyak), which for convenience are termed Paleo-Asiatic languages. Eskimo and Aleut languages may constitute a distinct group among these. The origin of the language of the Ket (Yenisey-Ostyak), who live in the middle reaches of Yenisey River, is still not clear. Hunting and fishing were the major means of livelihood of indigenous Siberian peoples, who follow six general patterns of life: (1) fishing and hunting people who move along rivers in the taiga forest region; (2) fishing people in permanent settlements along rivers and lakes; (3) sea mammal hunters on the Arctic coasts; (4) forest hunting and fishing people who make use of reindeer; (5) nomadic reindeer herders in the forests and tundra; and (6) stock farmers on the steppes and wooded steppes.

❻ TK 0480

❺ TK 0474

❼ TK 0478

❽ TK 0479

❺–❽ Reindeer Skin Articles (Sakhalin)
Articles of the Uilta and the Nivkhi (*from top left*: a small bag, tobacco pouch, small bag, and purse), all employing a special embroidery technique in which the thread does not show at the back of the tanned leather.

❾ Various Tools (Sakhalin)
Wooden articles of the Ainu and the Nivkhi. The shovel-shaped tools (*upper left*) are used to feed bear cubs that are kept in cages and used for ceremonial purposes.

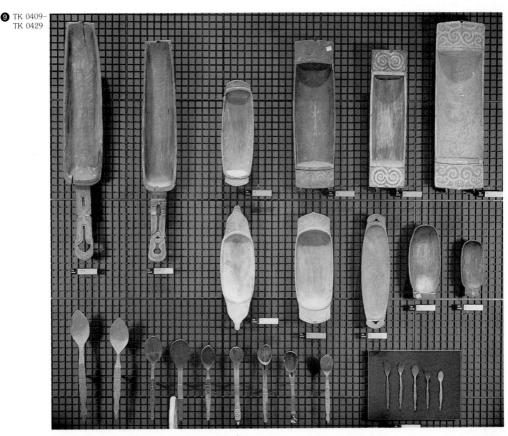

❾ TK 0409–
TK 0429

1 TK 0394-0397

3 TK 0297

2 TK 0393

4 TK 0303·0301

5 Birch Bark Containers (The Ul'chi, Siberia)
Everyday articles made by people along the lower reaches of the Amur River and decorated with symmetrical patterns.

6 Wooden Cups for Fermented Mare's Milk (The Yakut, Siberia)
The Yakut value their horses and enjoy fermented mare's milk. The feet on these cups are shaped like hooves.

5 TK 02
TK 02
TK 02

1 Hats and Gloves
Nivkhi and Uilta articles of reindeer and seal skin. Next to the ordinary warm hat (*left*) is one with an unusual shape.

2 Coat (replica) (The Nivkhi, Abashiri)
The Nivkhi hunt seals because their skins are warm and waterproof and can be put to many uses.

3 Woman's Formal Dress (The Ul'chi, Siberia)
The clothing of the fishing peoples along the lower reaches of the Amur River was made of the skin of fish such as salmon as well as silk and cotton from China and Japan.

4 Boots (*left*: The Yakut; *right*: The Negidal, Siberia)
Yakut boots are normally made of reindeer skin or horse-hide with a strip of cloth attached on the upper part.

6 TK 0278
TK 0279

The Cultures of East Asia

The area known as East Asia comprises China, Japan, and the Korean Peninsula. The northern and western parts of East Asia consist of arid steppes and deserts, whereas the eastern and southern regions—the most densely populated areas in the world—are humid regions affected by the monsoons.

In the semiarid regions of northern and western East Asia, swidden, or slash-and-burn, cultivation developed in ancient times, whereas in the steppes nomadism became the principal way of life. In contrast, the monsoon regions in the south and east saw the development of wet paddy farming at an early stage, and this gave rise to a culture centering around the cultivation of rice. This was later transmitted to Japan and became the basis of Japanese culture.

Chinese civilization, which evolved in the basin of the Yellow River before the fifteenth century B.C., subsequently spread to surrounding regions and became a great cultural influence on all of East Asia. As Chinese religion, thought, and technology spread, its writing system was also transmitted,

which led to a cultural area with a common form of writing.

In addition to independent languages such as Japanese, Korean, and Ainu, many families of languages and individual languages—among them, Sino-Tibetan (spoken by a large number of people), Altaic, Austro-Asiatic, Austronesian, Tai-Kadai (Daic), and Indo-European—are found in East Asia and have produced highly varied ethnic cultures. However, East Asia is seen as a single cultural entity because of the influence of Chinese civilization on the surrounding areas.

The exhibit on Japanese culture is the last of the exhibits on East Asia. The journey eastward across the world that began with Oceania comes to an end here. (Komei Sasaki)

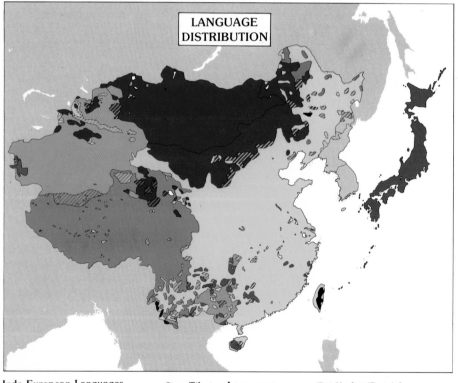

LANGUAGE DISTRIBUTION

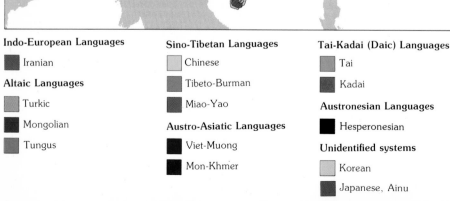

Indo-European Languages

▮ Iranian

Altaic Languages

▮ Turkic

▮ Mongolian

▮ Tungus

Sino-Tibetan Languages

▯ Chinese

▮ Tibeto-Burman

▮ Miao-Yao

Austro-Asiatic Languages

▮ Viet-Muong

▮ Mon-Khmer

Tai-Kadai (Daic) Languages

▮ Tai

▮ Kadai

Austronesian Languages

▮ Hesperonesian

Unidentified systems

▯ Korean

▮ Japanese, Ainu

The Culture of the Korean Peninsula

The Korean Peninsula lies to the south of the Yalu and Tumen rivers in the easternmost section of the Asian continent, and it is treated here together with Cheju Island and a number of other islands. Temperate forests of deciduous trees comprise the main vegetation on the peninsula, but subarctic forests are found in the north, and glossy-leaf forest regions in the extreme south.

From around 7000 to 6000 B.C., a hunting and fishing way of life changed to one centering on farming, and from 3000 to 2000 B.C. a distinct culture made its appearance on the peninsula. It is thought that before the unification of Korea in the tenth century B.C. there was intermingling among the various neighboring tribes. Although the Koreans are said to closely resemble the Japanese and the Manchus, through its many historical stages Korea absorbed the cultures of its neighbors to the north and west and created its own distinctive culture.

The Korean language is structurally similar to Japanese but is phonemically very different. Dialects also vary greatly from region to region, and the number of dialects as well as the different cultures reflect the complicated process by which ethnic groups were formed. Buddhism was introduced during the unified period from the Silla to the Koryŏ dynasties (7th–14th centuries), a time when the ruling class played a central role, and Confucianism came to be adopted during the early Yi dynasty (1392–1910). The influence of these two beliefs is still strong today. A distinctive faith combining indigenous shamanism and foreign religions also evolved among the common people.

The social structure depends on a family system called *munjung* or *chongchinghae*, based on strict patrilineal descent and the vertical relationship of the generations, and this forms the basis of all human relations and is evident in rites of passage, such as coming-of-age ceremonies, weddings, and funerals, as well as in festivals. The tradition of ancestral rites has also been relatively well preserved to the present day. In villages, which serve as regional focal points, social unity and community integration are strengthened by rituals and a system of mutually helping one another on a day-to-day basis.

Distinctive features of the culture of the Korean Peninsula are: (1) its multilayered cultural elements, drawn from both indigenous and foreign cultures, particularly Chinese; and (2) its bi-level class structure, with upper- and lower-class cultures. These two aspects are supported by the strong network of families and village communities. The Korean exhibit is organized around the themes of folk beliefs, performing arts, dress, food, housing, and Confucianism, and the culture is approached from both the spiritual aspect, including the performing arts, beliefs, and religious ceremonies, and the physical aspect, covering dress, food, and housing. (Tetsuo Sakurai)

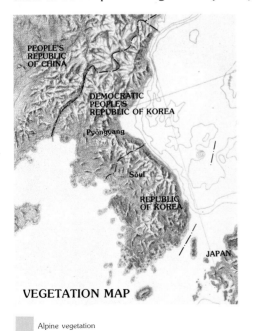

VEGETATION MAP

Alpine vegetation

Coniferous forest (subalpine zone, subarctic zone)

Temperate deciduous broad-leaf forest

Glossy-leaf forest (broad-leaf evergreen forest)

❶ HI 10001–10004

❶ **Changsŭng and Sotte** (Kyŏnggi-do, Republic of Korea)

A *changsŭng*, or carving of a face, and a *sotte*, or carving of a bird, are symbols of Korean shamanism and are placed at the entrance to a village as guardian deities.

❶ HI 10319

❸ HI 10328

❹ HI 10329

❷ HI 10320, etc.

Performing Arts, Beliefs, and Religious Ceremonies

Folk performing arts had their origins in everyday work activities and in the common people's enjoyment of sarcasm. The farmer's dance is typical of the former, and the masked play typical of the latter. At one time both types of performance had strong connections with Korean shamanism, which had deep roots in popular faith. In addition to widespread divination practices, belief in the *changsŭng* and *sotte*, the guardian spirits of the village, was also common, and both were closely tied to the supernatural. Even today there is strong interest in divination rites, particularly among Korean women. In contrast, the rites performed by men are strongly influenced by Confucianism, transmitted from China during the early Yi dynasty in the fifteenth century. Thus, Confucian and shamanistic rites merge in special ceremonies such as festivals and funerals, and it is not unusual to find both Confucian and shamanistic festivals in the same village. Ancestor worship is also important, following the Confucian precept of respect for one's elders, through which family ties are strengthened.

❶ Farmer's Dance Costumes (Republic of Korea)
Colorful strips of cloth are worn over the white costume, and the large drum, called a *changgo*, is hung around the neck, while other musical instruments are held in the hands.

❷–❹ Farmer's Dance Headgear (Republic of Korea)
In this dance, the two kinds of headgear are the cap and the hat decorated with flowers. The white cloth strings and chain attached to the metal knob on top of the cap swing around as the wearer moves.

❺–❾ Instruments for the Farmer's Dance
A trumpet called a *taepyŏngso* (❾) and small and large gongs (❺, ❻) and drums. The large *changgo* drum (❽) is hung around the neck and the small drum (❼), called a *sogo*, is held in the hand.

❿–⓫ Banners for the Farmer's Dance (Republic of Korea)
The tall banner, over five meters long, reads "The farmer is the foundation of the nation," and the small one bears the word "Law."

❿ HI 10333

⓫ HI 10318

❺ HI 10335

❻ HI 10334

❼ HI 10336
HI 10337

❾ HI 10342

❽ HI 10338

141

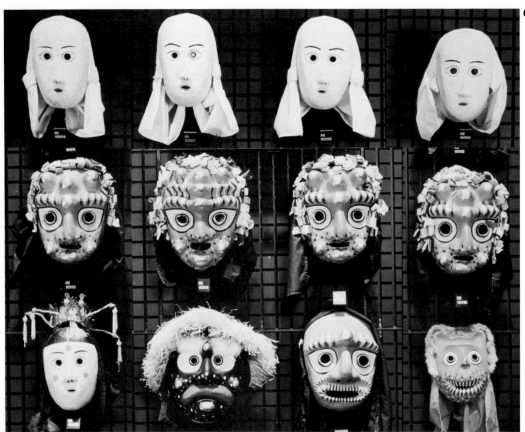

❶ HI 10005–
HI 10023

❷ HI 10026–
HI 10029

❸ HI 10030–
HI 10033

❶–❸ **Masks for Pongsan Masked Plays** (Democratic People's Republic of Korea)
These plays originated in Hwanghae-do district and are representative masked plays of the Korean Peninsula. The plays are in part satires on the upper classes of the Yi dynasty, such as aristocrats and priests.

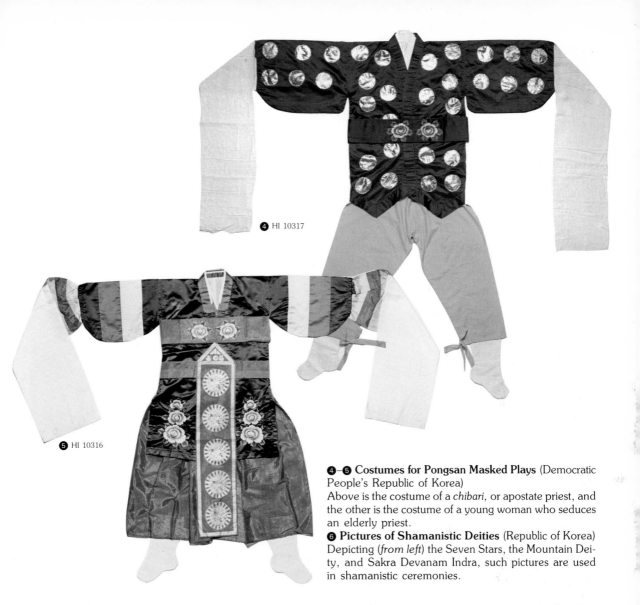

④ HI 10317

⑤ HI 10316

④–⑤ Costumes for Pongsan Masked Plays (Democratic People's Republic of Korea)
Above is the costume of a *chibari,* or apostate priest, and the other is the costume of a young woman who seduces an elderly priest.
⑥ Pictures of Shamanistic Deities (Republic of Korea)
Depicting (*from left*) the Seven Stars, the Mountain Deity, and Sakra Devanam Indra, such pictures are used in shamanistic ceremonies.

⑥ HI 10285

HI 10205–10225・10227

Dress, Food, and Housing

Today, both men and women in Korea wear Western attire, but the traditional dress for men was a basic combination of a *chŏgori* (jacket) and *paji* (voluminous trousers), and for women a *chŏgori* and *chima* (divided skirt). Even today, traditional clothing is frequently worn by women on ceremonial occasions. White is the color for somber ceremonies such as funerals, whereas bright reds, blues,

greens, and purples predominate in festive events. Korean food is also marked by strong contrasts, with the liberal use of strong-tasting seasonings such as garlic and red pepper. In housing, living space is functionally divided. Stones and tiles are used for building, and the *ondol*, or underfloor heating system, is a distinguishing feature of Korean houses.

144

❸ HI 10189–
HI 10193

❷ HI 10173

❹ HI 10044

❺ HI 10081 · 10082 · 10079 · 10076 · 10080

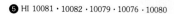

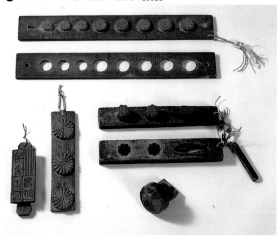

❼ HI 10152

❽ HI 10154

❻ HI 10084 · 10086–10088

❶ **Clothing for Rites of Passage** (Republic of Korea)
Special clothing is worn at rites of passage ceremonies.
The clothing at the top is worn by infants on their first
birthday. At the bottom are the wedding garments of a
bride and groom.
❷ **Cloth-beating Block** (Kyŏngsang-pukto, Republic of
Korea)
Used to squeeze out water and flatten the laundry.
❸ **Combs** (Hamgyŏng-namdo and P'yŏngan-namdo,
Democratic People's Republic of Korea)
❹ **Everyday Food** (replica)
A basic meal consists of grain, usually rice, with soup,
kimchi (pickled cabbage), and an array of side dishes.
❺ **Wooden Molds for Sweets and Rice Cakes** (Ch'ungch'ŏng-namdo, Republic of Korea)
❻ **Storage Jars** (Ch'ungch'ŏng-namdo, Republic of
Korea)
Used for storing soy sauce and soy bean paste.
❼ **Wooden Shoes** (P'yŏngan-namdo, Democratic People's Republic of Korea)
❽ **Ladies' Shoes** (Ch'ungch'ŏng-namdo, Republic of
Korea)

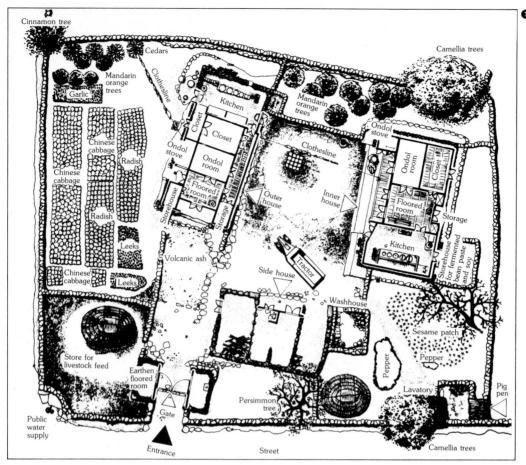

① HI 10055

- Cinnamon tree
- Cedars
- Mandarin orange trees
- Garlic
- Clothesline
- Kitchen
- Closet
- Closet
- Camellia trees
- Mandarin orange trees
- Chinese cabbage
- Radish
- Chinese cabbage
- Ondol stove
- Ondol room
- Clothesline
- Ondol stove
- Ondol room
- Closet
- Radish
- Storehouse
- Floored room
- Outer house
- Inner house
- Flooredroom
- Storage
- Leeks
- Storage
- Kitchen
- Storehouse for fermented bean paste and soy
- Chinese cabbage
- Volcanic ash
- Side house
- Tractor
- Leeks
- Washhouse
- Sesame patch
- Store for livestock feed
- Earthen floored room
- Pepper
- Pepper
- Persimmon tree
- Lavatory
- Pig pen
- Public water supply
- Gate
- Entrance
- Street
- Camellia trees

② Structure of an Ondol Floor

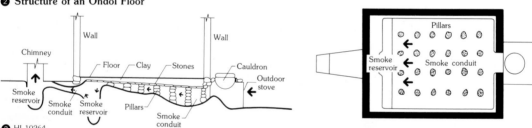

- Wall
- Wall
- Chimney
- Floor — Clay — Stones
- Cauldron
- Outdoor stove
- Smoke reservoir
- Smoke conduit
- Smoke reservoir
- Pillars
- Smoke conduit
- Pillars
- Smoke reservoir
- Smoke conduit
- Smoke reservoir
- Smoke conduit
- Pillars

③ HI 10264

4 HI 10149

6 HI 10108–
HI 10117

7 HI 10141
HI 10142

5 HI 10146·10145·10143·10144

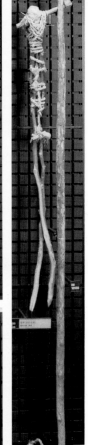

8 HI 10129·10128

9 HI 10138

❶ House on Cheju Island (Republic of Korea)
Such houses are characterized by the abundant use of
stone, and the thatched roofs are secured with ropes as
a precaution against strong winds. The basic floor plan
is of a three-roomed house, with a central room with a
wooden floor and a room on each side. This is the floor
plan of the model house in the central part of the display area.

❷ Structure of an Ondol Floor
The *ondol* is an excellent heating system in which smoke
from an outdoor stove is channeled through underfloor
conduits of stones or clay.

❸ Furniture (Republic of Korea)
Furniture from the head of the household's room, called
a *sarangbang*, modeled on that used in a Yi-dynasty
aristocrat's house.

❹ Back Basket (Chŏlla-namdo, Republic of Korea)

❺ Carrying Basket and Head Supports for Loads
The basket is from P'yŏngan-namdo (Democratic Peo-
ple's Republic of Korea). The supports are (*from left*) from
Kyŏngsang-pukto and Kyŏngsang-namdo (Republic of
Korea), and P'yŏngan-namdo (Democratic People's
Republic of Korea).

❻ Farm Tools (Republic of Korea)

❼ Winnows (Kyŏngsang-pukto, Republic of Korea)

❽ Fodder Shovels for Cattle (Kyŏngsang-namdo,
Republic of Korea)

❾ Hulling Pole (Kyŏngsang-pukto, Republic of Korea)

147

The Regional Cultures of China

The ethnic culture of the People's Republic of China is extremely varied, having been developed by as many as fifty-six different groups of people. The Han people form the largest group, and they are widely distributed over northeast, north, central, and southern China. The distribution of the Han and the fifty-five smaller groups is shown on the map opposite.

A general survey of China's racial groups shows that the Oroqen, Evenki, and Hezhen lived in forests and along rivers in the northeast, where the hunting and gathering tradition has been transmitted to this day. In the dry grasslands of the north and northwest dwell the Mongol, Kazakh, and Kirgiz, all of whom are nomadic. On the Tibetan Plateau to the west, the Zang (Tibetan) people, with a culture based on Tibetan Buddhism (Lamaism), engage in agriculture and stock-raising. Over a large area in the mountains of southwest China are dispersed many small groups, including the Yi, Miao, Yao, Bouyei, and Hani, each with its own traditional way of life. And in the plains of Guangxi, almost 13 million Zhuang engage in rice cultivation. However, the dominant ethnic group in China is the Han, whose origins are uncertain but who are thought to have emerged between 2000 to 1000 B.C. in the middle reaches of the Yellow River. The Han people later spread from the north to the northeast and then to central and southern China, bringing with them many aspects of their culture, such as language, government and social systems, religion, and thought.

In the Jiangnan region south of the Yangzi River, an agricultural way of life based on paddy agriculture was established in ancient times, even before the emergence of the Han. From this, and under later influence from the north, an advanced culture centering around rice cultivation was created in the region, and this was transmitted to Japan to become the basis of Japanese culture. The first objective of the China exhibit is to show the distinctive features of life in the Jiangnan region. Included are a typical rice farmer's house, a complete set of farm equipment, and a typical fishing boat from the middle Yangzi area.

The second focus of the display is the development of the walled city that was an important element in Chinese civilization. Representing city life is a model of a traditional city dwelling in Beijing, called a *si he yuan* (four-roomed compound). There is also a display on festivals and the performing arts, with emphasis on urban traditions transmitted by the Han people.

The third theme concerns the festivals enjoyed by the minority peoples of southern China, including the ritualized Dragon Boat Race of the Miao. Some minority cultures of southwestern China share many similarities with the basic culture of Japan, and the fourth objective of the China exhibit is the portrayal of the cultural characteristics of these minority peoples, showing traditional clothing and other objects related to everyday life. The fifth and last theme is the nature of life on the Tibetan Plateau and of cattle-raising in the grasslands of the north and northwest. To a certain extent, this display is a continuation of that on Central Asia, and is thus connected with the exhibits from neighboring regions. (Komei Sasaki)

Transport boats on a river in Jiangnan.

THE DISTRIBUTION OF MINORITY PEOPLES
IN
THE PEOPLE'S REPUBLIC OF CHINA
(from *Chinese Minority Peoples*, Renmin Publications, 1981)

Han	
Mongol	
Man	
Chaoxian	
Daur	
Ewenki (Evenki)	
Oroqen	
Hezhen	
Hui	
Dongxiang	
Tu	
Salar	
Yugur	
Bonan	
Uyghur (Uighur)	
Kazak (Kazakh)	

Kirgiz	
Xibe	
Tajik (Tadzhik)	
Uzbek	
Tatar	
Russ	
Zang	
Monba	
Lhopa	
Yi	
Qiang	
Bai	
Hani	
Dai (Tai)	

Lisu	
Va	
Lahu	
Naxi	
Jingpo	
Blang	
Nu	
Primmi	
Achang	
Jino	

Benglong	
Drung	
Miao	
Bouyei	
Dong	
Sui	
Gelao	
Zhuang	

Yao	
Mulam	
Maonan	
Gin	
Li	
Tujia	
She	
Gaoshan	

Note: On this map, names of peoples follow the official Chinese system of romanization. The widely accepted variants of some names that are adopted in the text are given in parentheses.

① HI 10528-10539・10545-10562・10540-10544

Festivals and Performing Arts

Over the ages, numerous festivals and performing arts have evolved in the vast area that is China, especially among the Han people, and these are apparent in such seasonal celebrations as the Spring Festival, the Qing Ming Festival (when ancestral graves are cleaned), and the Dragon Boat Festival. In Beijing, on the fifteenth day of the first lunar month, called *Yuan xiao* (Sending Off the Old Year), all houses are decorated with colorful dragon lanterns in celebration of the Festival of Lanterns. Lion dances, boat dances, and dragon dances are typical performances on this night. Opera and *shuo chang* (a popular entertainment

with narration and singing) have been extremely popular in China since the Ming (1368–1644) and Qing (1644–1911) dynasties. In all, there are over 300 regional types of drama, including Beijing opera, *bang zi* opera (which came to Beijing from Shanxi), *yang ge* opera of northern farm villages, *ping ju* opera of north and northeast China, *hua deng* opera of Yunnan farm villages, Guangdong opera, and Sichuan opera. Regional characteristics are apparent in the narrative arts of *shuo chang*, the *tan ci* (story-telling to the accompaniment of stringed instruments) of central China, and the *qin shu* (story-telling mainly in song, accompanied by

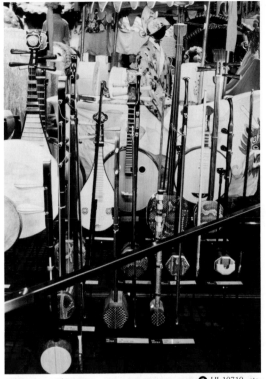

❻ HI 10686

❺ HI 10688

❹ HI 10691

musical instruments) of Shandong. Other performing arts include *pi ying xi* (shadow plays), *jia mian ju* (masked plays), singing, and various regional dances. Since the establishment of the People's Republic of China in 1949, each administrative district has a song and dance troupe that is responsible for the performing arts today, particularly music and dance.

❶ **Dolls**
On display are (*from top*) hand puppets from the puppet theater (The Han, Fujian Province), dolls (The Han, Hebei Province), and lions (The Han, Shanxi Province).
❷ **Han Musical Instruments** (The Han, Beijing)
Many musical instruments, including the *se*, a twenty-five-string plucked instrument somewhat similar to the zither, and a twelve-tone wind instrument, have been excavated from the Han tomb of Ma Wang Dui in Hunan Province. With classical instruments, folk instruments, and instruments improved since the 1949 revolution, the list of modern Han instruments is long, and many are closely related to Japanese instruments.
❸ **Musical Instruments of Minority Peoples**
In their variety of materials, shapes, and playing methods, these instruments reflect the environment and culture of the groups to which they belong. Typical examples are the elephant-leg drum of the Tai, the large three-stringed instrument of the Yi, reed instruments of the Dong and the Miao, and the horse-headed lyre of the Mongols.
❹ **Elephant-leg Drum** (The Tai, Yunnan Province)
This large, single-headed drum, which is slung from the shoulder, is essential to the ceremonies and festivals of the Tai.
❺ **Cattle Horn** (The Miao, Hunan Province)
❻ **Horn** (The Han, Beijing)
This horn is called a *suona*.

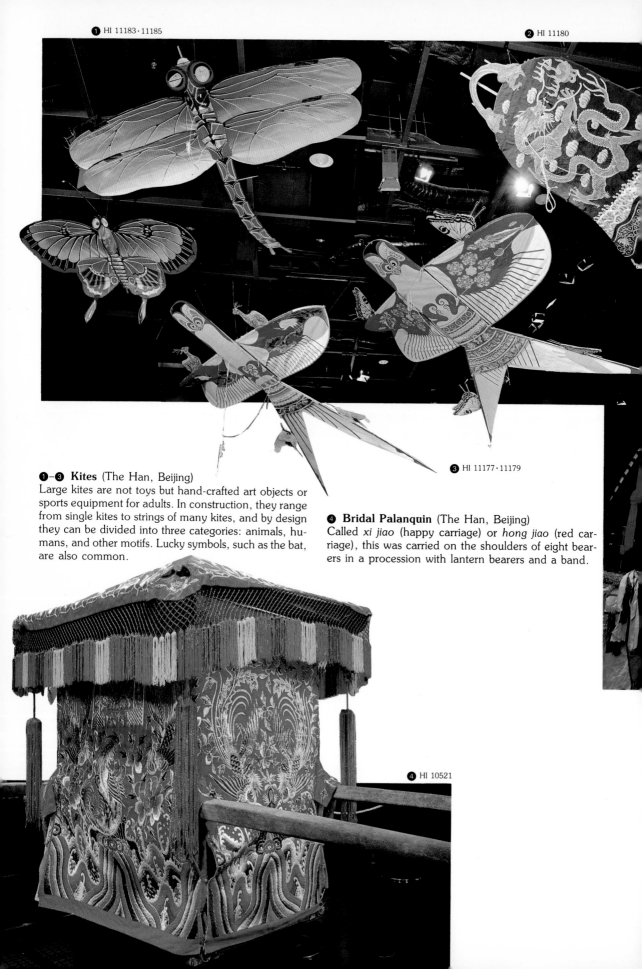

❶–❸ Kites (The Han, Beijing)
Large kites are not toys but hand-crafted art objects or sports equipment for adults. In construction, they range from single kites to strings of many kites, and by design they can be divided into three categories: animals, humans, and other motifs. Lucky symbols, such as the bat, are also common.

❸ HI 11177·11179

❹ Bridal Palanquin (The Han, Beijing)
Called *xi jiao* (happy carriage) or *hong jiao* (red carriage), this was carried on the shoulders of eight bearers in a procession with lantern bearers and a band.

❹ HI 10521

⑤ Dragon Dance (The Han, Beijing)
This dragon, supported by several people, is made to dance in the festivals on the first and fifteenth days of the Lunar New Year. Some dragons have electric lights so that each segment can be lit.

⑤ HI 10513

⑥ HI 10500

⑥ Dragon-head Boat (The Miao, Qingshui River, Guizhou Province)
This dragon head of the Miao has horns resembling those of the water buffalo. The hull is made of the hollowed-out trunk of a large tree such as a type of cedar or a paulownia, and miscanthus reeds are attached to the stern. From the twenty-fourth to the twenty-seventh of the fifth lunar month, dragon boat races are held in each village along the Qingshui River. About thirty paddlers stand in each 25-meter-long boat, which has a 2-meter-high dragon head, and in the bow sit a drummer and a man to beat the gong. The boats are differentiated by bright shades of red, blue, or yellow, and villages compete against one another. Processions of boats also go from village to village.

City Life

In China, cities were once enclosed within thick protective walls, but since the revolution of 1949 these city walls have been torn down to make way for traffic. Until the Ming dynasty, towns were laid out in the same way as agricultural villages. Urban apprentice systems imitated those of agricultural households, and the organization and work of guilds developed together with village communities. During the Qing dynasty, the small-scale commerce that appeared in towns was directly connected with farmers, but soon merchants began to dominate business and industry throughout the country. Modern commerce took root after the Opi-

um Wars in the mid-nineteenth century, but urban society continued to be semifeudalistic. Although the walls surrounding cities have disappeared and tall buildings have been constructed, the cities themselves have not been completely transformed. The necessity of preserving traditional styles of architecture is recognized, and in some places homes dating to the Ming and Qing dynasties still remain intact. For this display, Beijing has been taken as a representative city, and a model of a traditional city house known as a *si he yuan* (four-roomed compound) is exhibited.

❶–❷ Si he yuan (Four-Roomed Compound) (1/10 scale model) (The Han, Beijing).

This is a model of an actual house in Beijing, which today functions as a youth center. Since it is used for children's extracurricular activities, one section has been removed, but the fundamental elements of this style of house remain. The basic unit consists of four rooms—the main room, two side rooms, and a back room—built around an inner courtyard garden. The model on display is a larger version of this basic plan, with other gardens to the front and back of the inner garden, separated by carved gates. Where a series of gardens leads to the central one, they are named "first entry," "second entry," and so on. The outer walls provide privacy.

❶ HI 11051

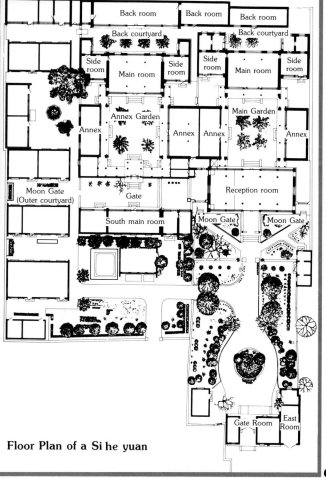

Floor Plan of a Si he yuan

❷ HI 11051

Life in Jiangnan

In the region to the south of the Yangzi River, called Jiangnan, an agricultural lifestyle based on rice cultivation was established at an early period. At the Hemudu site in Yuyao district, Zhejiang Province (a downstream region of the Yangzi River), rice cultivation is known to date from around 5000 B.C. Unhulled rice, horse chestnuts, peach stones, and gourds have been found at this site, as well as traces of wooden structures, including houses on stilts. There is evidence that animals such as pigs, dogs, and water buffalo were kept, and from the discovery of fish and deer bones, it is thought that fishing and hunting also flourished. Even today, the rice cultivation culture seen in this area remains little changed from long ago. Like the cultural history of this area, the formation of ethnic groups in Jiangnan is complex, for the region has been inhabited by various peoples from ancient times, although the Han eventually became dominant. There is a strong possibility that the rice cultivation that gave Japanese culture its characteristic features originated in Jiangnan.

❶ **Jiangnan Farmhouse** (reconstruction) (The Han, Jiangxi Province)
A typical farmhouse from the middle and downstream regions of the Yangzi River. The pine, crane, and deer motifs on the gate turret are invocations to the God of Wealth.

❷ **Fishing Boat and Equipment** (The Han, Jiangxi Province)
Called a *gou chuan* (hook boat) locally, this boat was constructed in the early 1920s and used on Lake Poyang, the largest freshwater lake in China. It carries fishing equipment such as a cast net, gill net, hand net, and longline. Almost twenty different species of fish are caught from such a boat, including whitebait and carp. Sails and

oars are used to propel the boat. The rain-cover consists of four layers of woven bamboo.

❸ **Incense Stand** (The Han, Jiangxi Province)
Placed at the far end of the entrance hall, such stands are used for venerating one's ancestors. Red strips of paper, on which were written such words as "the gods of heaven, earth, country, parent, and teacher," are pasted on the wall behind it.

❹ **Baskets, Rice Gruel Containers, and Steaming Basket** (The Han, Jinxian District and Leping District, Jiangxi Province)
Containers are either made of bamboo (for vegetables) or iron. The steaming basket (*bottom left*) is made of bamboo, and the rice gruel containers (*top left*) are of wood.

❷ HI 10826, etc.

❸ HI 10754, etc.

❹ HI 10772–10777

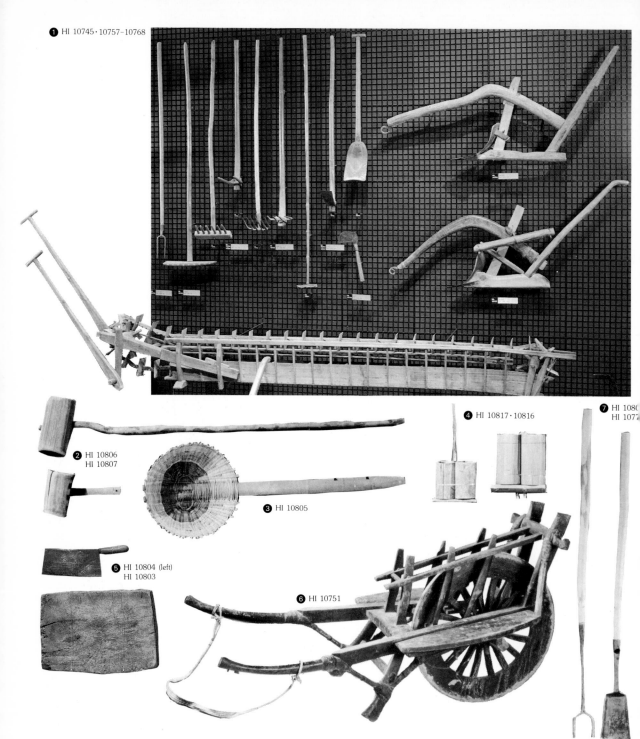

❶ HI 10745·10757–10768

❷ HI 10806
HI 10807

❸ HI 10805

❹ HI 10817·10816

❼ HI 1080
HI 1077

❺ HI 10804 (left)
HI 10803

❻ HI 10751

❶ Farm Equipment from Jiangnan (The Han, Jiang-xi Province)
These tools from a farm engaged in rice cultivation in a Jiangxi village include plows, a "dragon-bone wheel" for pumping water, and various hoes. Other tools include those for turning the soil and wooden receptacles for hulling rice.

❷ Ladles (The Han, Jinxian District, Jiangxi Province)
These are called *shui shao* (water ladles) and are used for scooping water from water jars.

❸ Rice Scoop (The Han, Jiangxi Province)
Called a *zhao li*, this bamboo ladle is used to scoop rice from a boiling pot of water for steaming—one method of cooking rice.

❹ Chopstick Stands (The Han, Jiangxi Province)
The stands are made from cylindrical lengths of bamboo. Chopsticks are also of bamboo and do not belong to any one person but can be used by any member of the family.

❺ Kitchen Chopper and Chopping Board (The Han, Jiangxi Province)

❻ Wheelbarrow (The Han, Jiangxi Province)
Known as a "red barrow," this is pushed after looping the rope around the neck. A bamboo basket or other container is tied on top of the shaft.

❼ Poker and Ash Shovel (The Han, Jiangxi Province)
The poker and ash shovel are used for clearing out the cooking stove that always occupies one corner of the kitchen.

158

Life in the Mountains

In southern China, the natural environment is extremely varied, and lifestyles are consequently diverse. From ancient times, minority peoples have inhabited the valleys there, the Yun-Gui Plateau (Yunnan and Guizhou provinces), where there are mountains between 1,000 and 2,000 meters high, and the Guangdong and Guangxi tablelands. Even today, each minority people carefully preserves its own language, costumes, arts, and religion. Originally, these were wandering peoples who lived mostly by slash-and-burn farming, but with the adoption of irrigation, most of them have settled down in one place. Peoples living here not only felled trees but, following ancient custom, also planted a variety of cedar. Houses on stilts, utilizing the rich forest resources, are common.

❽ Hulling Pole (The Zhuang, Guangxi Zhuang Autonomous Region)
Because the small pole swings around, this is a more effective tool than a single pole.
❾ Spade (The Yao, Guangxi Zhuang Autonomous Region)
❿ Digging Tool (The Yao, Hunan Province)
With the decline of slash-and-burn farming, such tools are now disappearing.
⓫ Winnow (The Hani, Yunnan Province)
This is one of many household items made of bamboo and wisteria, which grow in abundance in the mountains of the south.
⓬ Panicle Cutters
Used for harvesting ears of glutinous rice, which is preferred by mountain peoples and grown more commonly than non-glutinous rice.
⓭–⓮ Back Baskets
As wheeled vehicles are difficult to use in the mountains, baskets are the most convenient means for transporting goods. The basket with a board fitting on the shoulders is used by the Hani, and the other by the Yao.
⓯ Straw Raincoats and Bamboo Hats
These are worn by the Miao, Yao, Maonan, Dong, Zhuang, and Hani peoples, who live in regions of heavy rainfall that include Sichuan, Yunnan, Guizhou, Hunan, and Guangxi provinces.

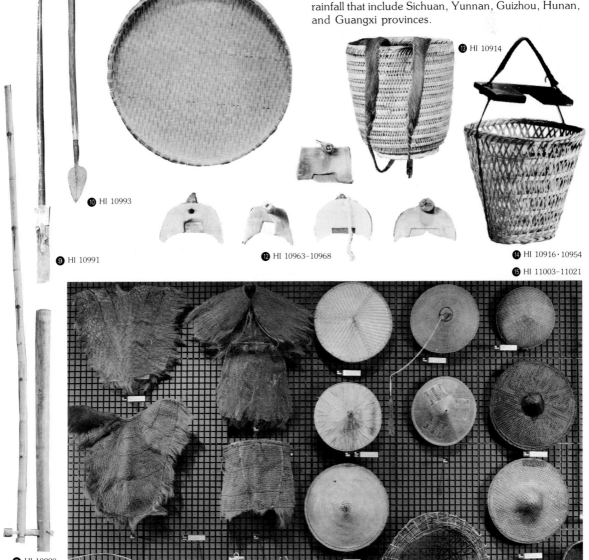

⓫ HI 10986
⓭ HI 10914
❿ HI 10993
❾ HI 10991
⓬ HI 10963–10968
⓮ HI 10916·10954
⓯ HI 11003–11021
❽ HI 10998

159

❶ HI 10860, etc.

❷ HI 11052

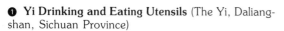

❶ **Yi Drinking and Eating Utensils** (The Yi, Daliang-shan, Sichuan Province)
A set of lacquerware—including trays, bowls, soup bowls, seasoning containers, spoons, and wine cups—distinguished by the use of red, yellow, and black. The main meat in Yi cooking is pork, and the people's love of wine is evident from the elaborately worked wine cups. The type of wine container displayed (*third row from front*) has a head, body, and foot. The flat circular body is made by fitting the two halves together, and a long bamboo pipe is inserted from the bottom of the leg into the body. To fill the container, it is turned upside down and wine is poured through the bamboo pipe; because the mouth of the pipe is higher than the level of the wine, this will not leak out even when the container is righted. Wine is poured out through the bamboo pipe sticking out of the body.

❷ **Miao Clothing** (The Miao, Guizhou Province)
Miao clothing, worn by people spread over a wide area, varies according to region, but embroidered patterns of dragons and phoenixes are common to all.

❸ **Yao Clothing** (The Yao, Yunnan Province)
Yao clothing also differs by region, and the differences in head ornaments are especially striking.

❸ HI 11056

Life on the Tibetan Plateau

The Tibetan Plateau, with an average altitude of about 4,000 meters, has both large lakes in Qinghai Province and the Manaslu Mountains, and it is also the source of the major rivers of Asia—the Yangzi, Yellow, Mekong, and Brahmaputra rivers. Most of the inhabitants of the plateau are Zang (Tibetans), with a few Han and Hui people in the cities, and Monba and Lhopa peoples in the southeastern area. Through its long period of isolation, the region has developed its own culture, including the Tibetan language, the Tibetan calendar, and a distinctive marriage system. People live by raising sheep, goats, and yaks for milk, butter, and meat, and clothing is made from their skins and their wool. Spiritual life centers on the native Bon religion and Tibetan Buddhism, or Lamaism, which was adopted after the eighth century, but with the establishment of the Tibetan Autonomous Region in 1965, society and culture were modernized and transformed.

❹ Prayer Wheel (The Zang, Tibetan Autonomous Region)
This prayer wheel has an invocation to the principal Tibetan protective deity inscribed on its surface.

❺ Tsampa Holders and Tea Bag (The Zang, Tibetan Autonomous Region)
Leather bags for *tsampa* (barley flour) and an embroidered cloth bag for *chapaka* (lumps of tea).

❻ Tea Maker (The Zang, Tibetan Autonomous Region)
Brick tea is boiled and poured into this churn, called a *dongmo*, then salt and butter are added and the mixture is churned.

❼ Articles of Silver (The Zang, Tibetan Autonomous Region)
In the middle row at left is a snuff holder, and in the back row are, from the left, a teacup with a lid, a set of teacups, and a wine cup called a *phupor*. Before the 1949 revolution, these dishes were used by the upper classes and in temple rituals. The *phupor* was frequently used as a container for holy water.

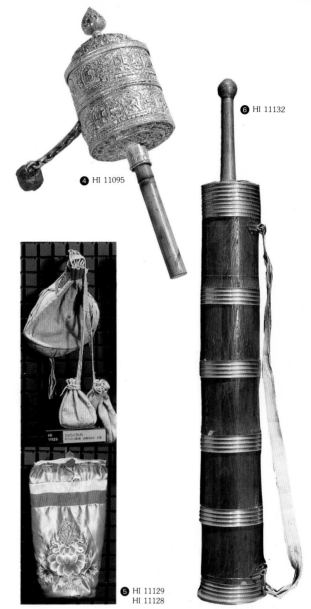

❹ HI 11095

❻ HI 11132

❺ HI 11129
HI 11128

❼ HI 11102–
HI 11111

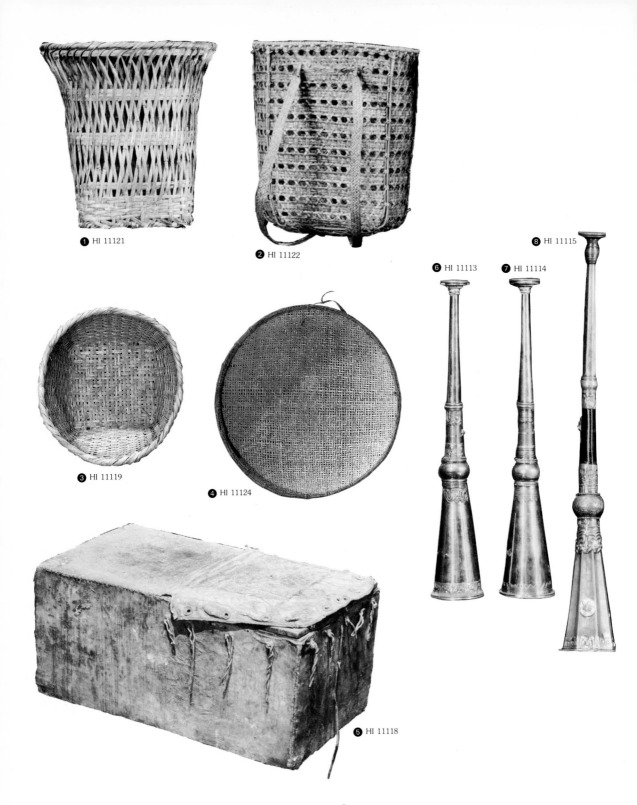

① HI 11121
② HI 11122
③ HI 11119
④ HI 11124
⑤ HI 11118
⑥ HI 11113
⑦ HI 11114
⑧ HI 11115

①–② **Back Baskets** (The Lhopa, Tibetan Autonomous Region)
Baskets like these are found in Tibet, Nepal, and Bhutan, with some types supported by a strap around the forehead.

③ **Vegetable Basket** (The Lhopa, Tibetan Autonomous Region)

④ **Sieve** (The Zang, Tibetan Autonomous Region)
A sieve used in hulling wheat and barley, primarily in the Kham region.

⑤ **Sutra Holder** (The Zang, Tibetan Autonomous Region)
Temporary storage for sutras and printing blocks. To store a sutra more permanently, it is placed between two thin boards on a shelf.

⑥–⑧ **Bugles** (The Zang, Tibetan Autonomous Region)
Used in Tibetan Lamaist ceremonies, the longer ones, up to four meters in length, are played in pairs, and the smaller ones accompany them.

Life on the Grasslands

The broad dry expanse extending from the Inner Mongolian Autonomous Region to the Xinjiang Uighur Autonomous Region is a patchwork of deserts and grasslands, with a number of high mountain ranges running east to west, such as the Yin Shan, Altai Shan, and Tian Shan. South of the Tian Shan Mountains lies the Talimu basin, where farming has been undertaken in scattered oasis areas since early times. Located on the fringes of ancient Chinese civilization, this region experienced the rise and decline of a very different culture. The grasslands were primarily inhabited by nomads who raised stock for their milk, meat, and skins. The Mongolians, as well as the Turks, Uighur, Kazakh, and Kirgiz were nomads, but the nomadic way of life is slowly dying out because the conditions supporting it have disappeared. In recent times, more than half the population of the region are Han people.

❾ Copper Trays and Pitchers (The Uighur, Xinjiang Uighur Autonomous Region)
Pitchers with a beak-like spout are used mainly for washing the hands and are found from Central to West Asia. Pitchers with a straight, vertical spout (*front, second from left*) are for drinking water. The trays are used for serving food and fruit.

❾ HI 11078–11079
HI 11070–11075
HI 11077

❷ HI 11063

❸ HI 11057

❹ HI 11068

❺ HI 11064

❶ **Carpets** (The Uighur, Xinjiang Uighur Autonomous Region)
From the left, these traditional designs are called *chachima*, *anarugyuru*, and *keruku*. At the far right is a felt rug.

❷ **Camel Saddle** (Inner Mongolian Autonomous Region, Xinjiang Uighur Autonomous Region)
Made of canvas-covered felt and placed between the humps of Bactrian camels.

❸–❹ **Horse Saddles** (❸ The Kazakh, Xinjiang Uighur Autonomous Region; ❹ The Mongols, Inner Mongolian Autonomous Region)
Horses are still an important means of transportation, and birch is often used for the saddle frames.

❺ **Saddlebag** (The Kazakh, Xinjiang Uighur Autonomous Region)
Made of carpet, although such bags are usually of woven cotton. This is placed on a donkey's or horse's back.

The Culture of the Ainu

The Ainu lived in the expanses of broad-leafed deciduous forest in Hokkaidô, the southern areas of Sakhalin (Karafuto) Island, the Kuril (Tisima) Islands, and the northern areas of Honsyû, the main island of Japan. This region was not homogenous, however, for broadly speaking there developed three regional groups with their own characteristics, cultural elements, and dialects—the Sakhalin, the Hokkaidô, and the Kuril groups, as shown on the map. In winter, these areas are all snowbound, and the social structure, ways of thought, and daily life of the Ainu developed in response to the climate and from their activities of hunting, fishing, and gathering plants. The resultant Ainu culture was rich in originality and creativity.

Even before their incorporation into modern Japan when the Meiji government was formed in 1868, the Ainu people and culture were not completely isolated because of their contacts with their neighbors through trade and other activities. In particular, the Sakhalin and Hokkaidô Ainu took furs and marine products to the lower reaches of the Amur River on the Asian continent—at that time under the control of the Qing dynasty (1644–1911)—and there exchanged them for brocade and necklaces of treasured blue glass beads. These products were used by the Ainu both as ornamentation and for trading, and thus came into the hands of Japanese merchants who ventured north in boats bearing lacquerware and cotton kimono. In this way, goods from the Amur River region made their way into Japan, where they were highly prized.

The first section of the Ainu exhibit consists of articles depicting the flourishing trade between Honsyû and the continent. A selection of Ainu clothes is also on display and demonstrates differences among regional groups regarding materials, needlework, and design motifs. Such garments are the Sakhalin *tetarape*, made from nettles, the feathered robe of the Kuril Ainu, and the *attus* robe of the Hokkaidô Ainu.

The next section concerns the Ainu house, the focus of daily life. The exhibit is structured so that visitors can examine Ainu life in ever-widening circles, from clothing and personal ornaments to outdoor activities such as hunting and fishing, the gathering of plants, and millet cultivation. An elaborate model with such elements as the main house, the outdoor sacred area, a storehouse with raised floor, a bear cage, a water-drawing site, a garden, and the surrounding forest bestows an appreciation of Ainu life in its environment.

The well-known Ainu *iyomante* (bear-spirit ceremony) is the subject of the last display, showing the outdoor sacred space and such ritual objects as a *sapaunpe* (sacred crown), *heperay* (flowered arrows), *ikupasuy* (prayer-sticks), and *inaw* (shaved-wood objects). The *iyomante* ceremony is held among the peoples of northern Siberia and is important to basic Ainu culture. The deep relationship between the Ainu people and Japanese culture is suggested by the display of Ainu shaved-wood objects, called *kezurikake* in Japanese. (Kazuyoshi Ohtsuka)

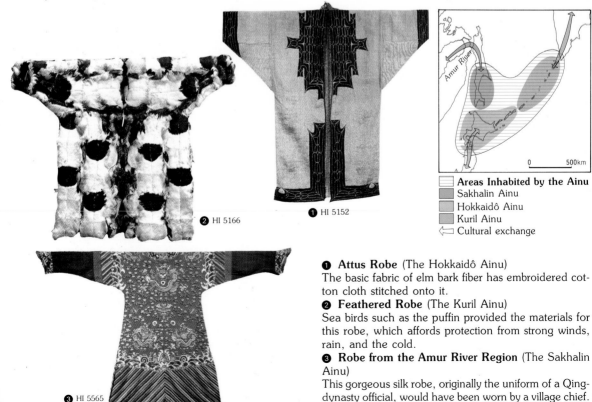

❷ HI 5166

❶ HI 5152

❸ HI 5565

Areas Inhabited by the Ainu
Sakhalin Ainu
Hokkaidô Ainu
Kuril Ainu
⬅ Cultural exchange

0　　500km

❶ **Attus Robe** (The Hokkaidô Ainu)
The basic fabric of elm bark fiber has embroidered cotton cloth stitched onto it.
❷ **Feathered Robe** (The Kuril Ainu)
Sea birds such as the puffin provided the materials for this robe, which affords protection from strong winds, rain, and the cold.
❸ **Robe from the Amur River Region** (The Sakhalin Ainu)
This gorgeous silk robe, originally the uniform of a Qing-dynasty official, would have been worn by a village chief.

Ainu Houses and Daily Life

When the Ainu built their houses, they chose sunny places that were sheltered from floods and avalanches, yet were near flowing water necessary for drinking. Regional differences can be seen in the materials used for roofs and walls: in southern Hokkaidô, including the Hidaka area, miscanthus was the main material; in northern Hokkaidô, such as the Asahikawa region, houses were made of bamboo grass; and in eastern Hokkaidô and on Sakhalin, tree bark was used. A married couple usually lived together with their unmarried children in one house. A village, called a *kotan*, was the basic unit for cooperative work and the center of daily activities and ritual. The village chief was chosen by members of the *kotan* and played a central role in religious celebrations and in maintaining social order. Each *kotan* had its own territory, or *iwor*, which provided all the natural daily necessities: men caught animals and fish with bows and arrows and traps, and women stripped bark from trees and gathered fruit and nuts. Entering another *iwor* was strictly forbidden, and if this rule was violated, compensation had to be made in the form of valued objects. For the Ainu, the *iwor* was their world, and within it they were essentially self-sufficient.

❶ **Ainu House and Surroundings** (scale model) (Nibutani, Hokkaidô)
A traditional Ainu homestead centered around the main house, called a *cise*. In the most common arrangement, to the east of the main house was a sacred area, to the southeast were a bear cage and a storehouse with a raised floor, to the south was an open space, and to the west were separate toilets for men and women.

❷ **Inside the Main House** (reconstruction) (Hidaka District, Hokkaidô)
The main house consists of one long room built on an east–west axis, with a sunken hearth in the middle of the floor. The most important guest sits on the patterned mat at the east end of the hearth, with the owner of the house to the guest's right. There is a sacred *rorunpuyar* (god-window) in the wall (*right*), and the protective deity of the house is enshrined in the northeast corner. Next to this is the treasure corner, with lacquer vessels and swords.

Ainu Occupations

Almost all the materials used by the Ainu for food, clothing, and houses were found in nature, and Ainu life centered around hunting, fishing, and gathering plants. Crops like millet were also cultivated in small plots, but this was secondary, since Ainu society was essentially a hunting and gathering one. Deer were important as they were easily caught and were thus a dependable source of food, and salmon was another basic food. Other animals, such as rabbits, foxes, and martens, were hunted for their meat and skins, and marine animals sought included seals, porpoises, and toothed whales. Bows and arrows, spears, and many kinds of traps were used for hunting on land, and toggle-headed harpoons testify to Ainu prowess in hunting marine animals and large fish at sea. Trout and salmon were the principal fishes caught, and for these a special hooked harpoon was often used. While the men hunted and fished, Ainu women gathered plants, and the root of a species of lily, called *turep*, was an important food.

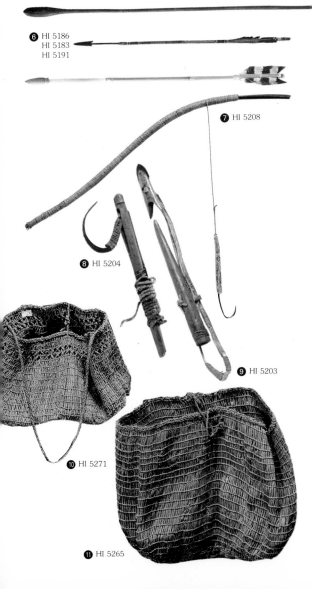

❸ Quiver (Hokkaidô)
This quiver, which is slung across the back and shoulders with a string, held arrows for hunting in the mountains. The quiver is made from a branch that is split in half, hollowed out, and joined together again. Cherry bark was wound around the outside to strengthen it.

❹ Small Knife (Akan, Hokkaidô)
This *makiri* knife was used for shaving sticks into *inaw* (shaved-wood objects), for hollowing out wooden bowls, and for making delicate carvings. An Ainu man was judged by his skill with a small knife.

❺ Mountain Knife (Hokkaidô)
This knife always hung at a man's waist whenever he was hunting or fishing, and was used to cut branches and kill game.

❻ Arrows (Hokkaidô)
The arrow at the top knocked down birds, such as ducks, in flight. The center arrow has an iron tip. The arrow at the bottom has a bamboo tip, which was dressed with poison.

❼ Fishing Hook (Sakhalin)
Used for winter sea fishing, when a hole was cut in the ice and this hook lowered into it. Red cloth was attached to the top of the lead weight to serve as a lure.

❽ Hooked Harpoon (Hokkaidô)
Mainly used from a boat or from the bank to catch trout and salmon swimming upstream. When the end of the wooden shaft struck a fish, the hook on the shaft rotated over the fish to embed itself in the other side.

❾ Toggle-headed Harpoon (Sakhalin)
This type of harpoon would not dislodge once it entered the body of the animal, and even toothed whales were caught with it.

❿–⓫ Woven Bags (Hokkaidô)
The inner bark of trees was finely shredded and woven into bags that have a strap so they can be carried on the back. Varied in size and shape, and with a range of patterns created by different weaving techniques, these bags were used especially by women collecting lily roots and other wild plants.

Ainu Beliefs

The Ainu believed that there are spirits in all things—people, tools, and objects both natural and man-made. Such spirits are immortal, and death is seen as the way to an eternal utopian existence. In the *iyomante* ceremony, a bear that has been carefully raised is killed in order to release the spirit from the bear's body and send it back to the spirit world. In other words, the bear spirit cannot return to the other world unless it sheds its bodily form, and the meat and skin of the bear are regarded as gifts from the gods to the people. In return, the Ainu erect *inaw* (shaved-wood objects), recite prayers, and offer saké, rice cakes, and other gifts to the gods. In this way, human beings and the deities who bestow the blessings of nature seek to coexist through the medium of ritual. The Ainu invoked their deities daily and prayed that the supply of necessities for daily life would never end. They regarded their deities as essentially the same as human beings, and when harm befell someone or things did not go as hoped, the Ainu would become angry with their deities and threaten not to worship them.

❶ Bear-shaped Deity (Sakhalin)
It was believed that the owner of this tree root, in which the bear deity resides, would be successful in hunting.
❷ Albatross-headed Deity (Nibutani, Hokkaidô)
Believed to protect human beings from evil spirits that bring illness.
❸ Turtle-headed Deity (Sizunai, Hokkaidô)
Used in rites to bring rain. When fire broke out, people also prayed to this deity to bring the fire under control.
❹–❺ Ikupasuy and Kikeuspasuy
When praying to deities, saké is put on the tip of an *ikupasuy* (prayer-stick) and it is presented as an offering, thus playing the role of an emissary bearing prayers to the deities. In the *iyomante* ceremony, *kikeuspasuy* (shaved prayer-sticks) of unpainted wood, bearing the carved symbol of the household supervising the ritual, are used.
❻ Sacred Headband (Hokkaidô)
Worn by men during the *iyomante* ceremony, such a carved wooden bear or wolf had real bear claws attached to the front.

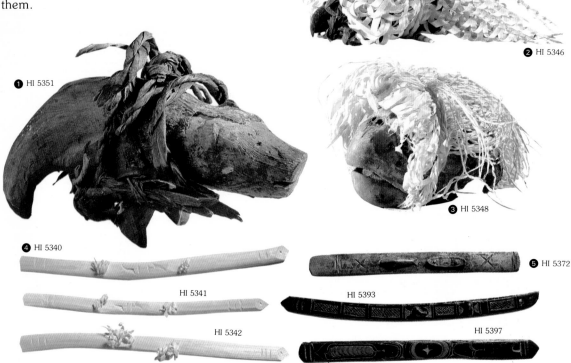

❷ HI 5346

❶ HI 5351

❸ HI 5348

❹ HI 5340

HI 5341

HI 5342

❺ HI 5372

HI 5393

HI 5397

❻ HI 5318

❼ Sacred Area (Nibutani, Hokkaidô)
Outside every Ainu house is a sacred area where *inaw* (shaved-wood objects) are lined up in rows. These are for the *iyomante* ceremony, and they are placed in the following order: (*from left*) inaw deity, farming deity, tree deity, hunting deity, bear deity (decorated with a bear skull), and water deity. To the extreme left is a low altar for worshiping family ancestors.
❽ Flowered Arrows (Asahikawa, Hokkaidô)
The tip is painted black, then carved and decorated with red cloth. During the *iyomante* ceremony, these blunt arrows are shot at the bear as a way of greeting its spirit.

❼ HI 5345

ARRANGEMENT OF *INAW* FOR THE *IYOMANTE* CEREMONY

| *Inaw* for ancestors | *Inaw* deity Farming deity | Tree deity | Hunting deity | Bear deity | Water deity |

❽ HI 5335

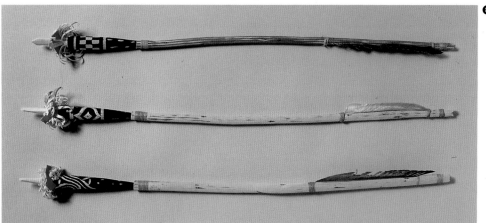

The Culture of Japan

The Japanese archipelago, which gave birth to Japanese culture, stretches 3,500 kilometers north to south along the eastern edge of the Asian continent. Its climatic zones range from subarctic to subtropical, and in its great variety of natural environments local cultures developed under the influence of neighboring cultures.

Situated at the eastern edge of the Asian continent, the Japanese archipelago was steadily influenced by the cultures of China and Korea, but nevertheless a distinct Japanese culture took shape on these islands. The exhibit on Japan re-creates the traditional lifestyles of the Japanese around two concepts: *hare* and *ke*. *Hare* is the cycle of annual religious events and rites of passage, as well as the arts related to them. In "Festivals and Performing Arts," a selection of artifacts used in religious rites, festivals, and performing arts allows visitors to sample the excitement of a festival.

Ke encompasses all aspects of daily life. The "Japanese Houses" exhibit displays typical dwellings from different areas of Japan to introduce cultures that have been nurtured by local environments

and climatic conditions. In addition, the plurality of Japanese culture is conveyed through collections of tools and objects in such exhibits as "Boats and Fishing Tools," "Hunting and Mountain Work," "Tools from Daily Life," and "Farming and Transportation Tools," which demonstrate the variety of lifestyles and occupations in farming, mountain, and fishing communities.

Many objects associated with traditional Japanese lifestyles have been disappearing in the last few years, but those on exhibit can still be found on the fringes of contemporary life. Until quite recently they were used on an everyday basis, and through them we can appreciate underlying motifs in Japanese culture that are difficult to perceive in modern society. (Takeshi Moriya)

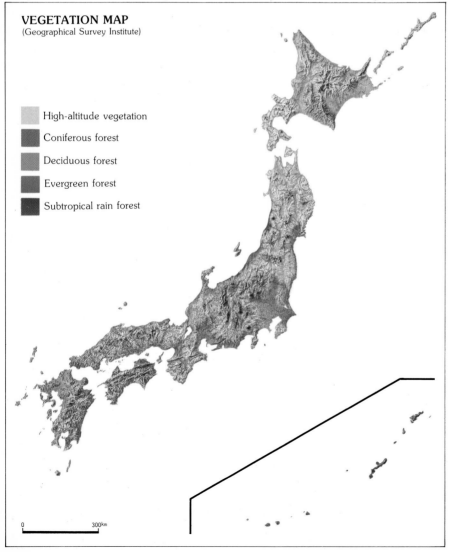

VEGETATION MAP
(Geographical Survey Institute)

High-altitude vegetation

Coniferous forest

Deciduous forest

Evergreen forest

Subtropical rain forest

0   300km

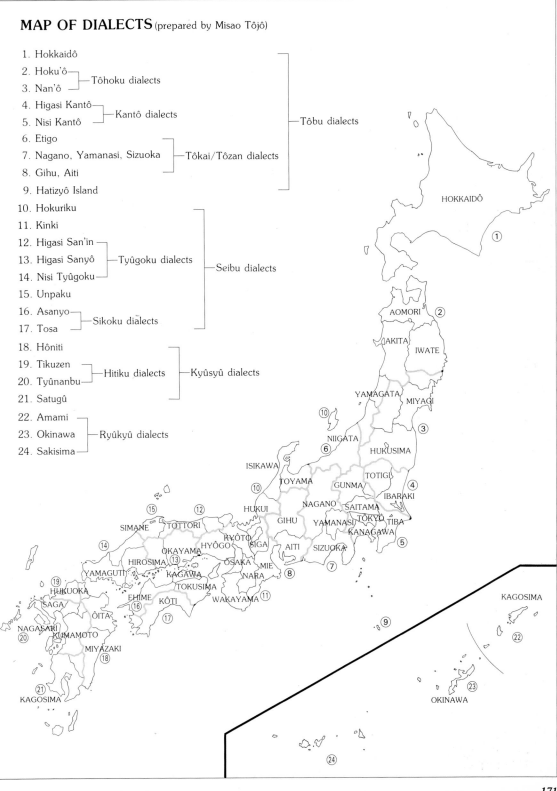

MAP OF DIALECTS (prepared by Misao Tôjô)

1. Hokkaidô
2. Hoku'ô ┐
   ├ Tôhoku dialects
3. Nan'ô ┘
4. Higasi Kantô ┐
   ├ Kantô dialects
5. Nisi Kantô ┘
6. Etigo
7. Nagano, Yamanasi, Sizuoka ┐
   ├ Tôkai/Tôzan dialects
8. Gihu, Aiti ┘
9. Hatizyô Island
10. Hokuriku
11. Kinki
12. Higasi San'in ┐
13. Higasi Sanyô ├ Tyûgoku dialects
14. Nisi Tyûgoku ┘
15. Unpaku
16. Asanyo ┐
   ├ Sikoku dialects
17. Tosa ┘
18. Hôniti
19. Tikuzen ┐
   ├ Hitiku dialects
20. Tyûnanbu ┘
21. Satugû
22. Amami ┐
23. Okinawa ├ Ryûkyû dialects
24. Sakisima ┘

Tôbu dialects

Seibu dialects

Kyûsyû dialects

HOKKAIDÔ ①

AOMORI ②
AKITA
IWATE
YAMAGATA
MIYAGI
⑩
NIIGATA
⑥
HUKUSIMA
③
ISIKAWA
TOYAMA
GUNMA
TOTIGI
IBARAKI ④
⑩
HUKUI
NAGANO
SAITAMA
GIHU
YAMANASI
TÔKYÔ
TIBA
KANAGAWA
⑤
⑮
⑫
SIMANE
TOTTORI
RYÔTO
SIGA
AITI
SIZUOKA
⑭
OKAYAMA
HYÔGO
OSAKA
MIE
⑦
HIROSIMA ⑬
KAGAWA
NARA
⑧
YAMAGUTI
TOKUSIMA
⑲
HUKUOKA
EHIME
WAKAYAMA
⑪
SAGA
⑯
KÔTI
⑨
ÔITA
⑰
NAGASAKI
KUMAMOTO
⑳
MIYAZAKI
⑱
㉑
KAGOSIMA

KAGOSIMA
㉒
OKINAWA
㉓

㉔

Festivals and Performing Arts

The three stages of a Japanese festival—greeting the deities, celebrating with them, and sending them off—have given rise to many symbolic forms. Some of these summon the deities, some provide a place for them to rest, and others delimit sacred space, and through the medium of folk performances such forms have profoundly influenced stage performances. The concept and function of many elements in Japanese performing arts—such as objects carried on the back, held in the hand, or covering the head—can only be explained in relation to festival artifacts. The masks and costumes and the wide selection of dolls on display may be regarded as local embodiments of the Japanese people's image of their deities, and they also provide clues as to how the performing arts developed. Most of the objects on display are unsophisticated, but the superb palanquins and carts that served as vehicles for the deities developed in conjunction with advanced craft techniques.

❶ **Deer Dance Masks and Costumes** (Tôno, Iwate Prefecture)
The *Sisi-odori* is a type of dance that imitates deer, and it occurs throughout the northeastern part of Honsyû. *Sisi* originally meant "beast," and in this dance these masks are thought to symbolize visiting deities from the mountains.

❶ HI 0753
HI 0752
HI 0751

② HI 2403

③ HI 2402

❷ Drum Platform (Niihama, Ehime Prefecture)
This large "mountain cart," which holds a drum behind
its richly embroidered curtains, was originally carried on
the shoulders of thirty or forty men, but in recent years
wheels have been attached so such carts can be pulled.
This type of drum platform is found throughout the Inland Sea area.

❸ Palanquin (Tôkyô)
A sacred palanquin is a miniature shrine containing the
sintai (literally, "body of a deity") that is carried around
the neighborhood of a shrine during a festival. This one,
made of zelkova wood with a roof in the Chinese gabled
style, was made in Asakusa in the early Syôwa period
(1926–89) and belonged to a shrine in Nihonbasi.

❹ Neputa (Hirosaki, Aomori Prefecture)
The festival called Neputa in Hirosaki (and Nebuta in
Aomori) is held in early August to rid people of the spirits
that cause sleepiness. The fan-shaped part, with paint-
ings of warriors and beautiful women, is peculiar to the
Hirosaki festival.

❹ HI 2031

173

❶ HI 2296, etc.

❷ HI 1048

❸ HI 1002

❹ HI 2837

❺ HI 2433 (left)
HI 2434

6 HI 2516, etc.

❶ Ropes

Simenawa (literally, "twisted rope") define the boundaries of sacred space, and are usually hung on the gateways to shrines or at the approach to a village. They are also often used as New Year's decorations in private homes. The *yokozuna* (*to the left of the objects in the photograph*), which is the ceremonial belt of twisted rope worn by the highest-ranking *sumô* wrestlers, and the *niô-dasuki* (*front, far left*), the cord used to tie up the sleeves of a Kabuki actor, can be regarded as developed forms of *simenawa*. The wedding decoration of a pine tree (*front, right*) and the *dôsozin* mask (*center*) are noteworthy for being made of straw.

❷ Mask from the Zyûgoya Festival (Yoron Island, Kagosima Prefecture)

Such masks are worn on this island near Okinawa on the evening of the fifteenth day of the eighth lunar month, when dances are performed as prayers for a bountiful harvest.

❸ New Year's Deities (Oga, Akita Prefecture)

On the evening of Little New Year (originally the night of the first full moon), young men wear these *namahage* masks to frighten children and young women.

❹ Hana Maturi Masks (Sakaki Oni) (Kitasitara, Aiti Prefecture)

Demons represent the spirits of evil in the Setubun Festival, held on the eve of the first day of spring according to the lunar calendar, but originally they were a frightening manifestation of the life force.

❺ Symbolic Halberds (Iwaki, Hukusima Prefecture)

A "dew-clearer," carrying such small halberds, appears in the Gohôden Dengaku ritual of Iwaki, which was originally a dance associated with rice cultivation. The crow represents the ocean, and the rabbit the mountains.

❻ Hand-held Objects

Many different objects are held in the hands for the sacred dance known as *kagura*, including fans, *hei* (paper strips on sticks), bells, swords, axes, and bows and arrows.

6 HI 2516, etc.

175

① HI 1076

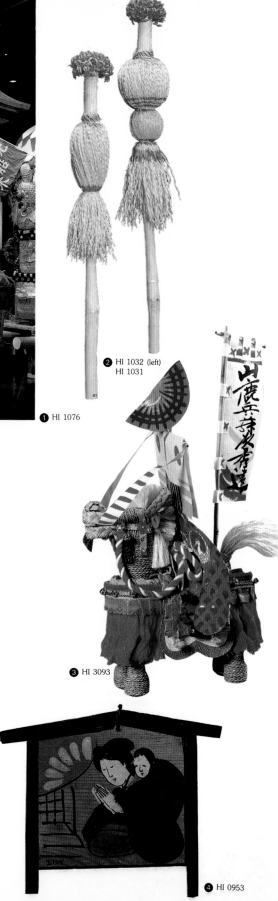

② HI 1032 (left)
HI 1031

③ HI 3093

④ HI 0953

① **Hiki-yama** (Takatuki, Siga Prefecture)
Children perform *kyôgen* (comic plays) and Kabuki—
traditional dramatic forms—on these *hiki-yama* (pulled
floats) during the Spring Festival.

② **Bonten** (Kakunodate, Akita Prefecture)
The *bonten* of this area are a type of shaved-wood figure.
On Little New Year (the night of the first full moon), children carrying them circle the homes of newly married
couples as an invocation for the birth of good children.

③ **Hassaku Horse** (Asiya, Hukuoka Prefecture)
On the first day of August, in families with a baby under
one year old, it is the custom in this region to present
a boy with a straw horse and a girl with a doll made of
sweets.

④ **Ema** (Sinobu, Saitama Prefecture)
Ema (literally, "picture horses") are votive tablets popular since the seventeenth century, when they were mass-
produced and sold in shops. The pictures are often rid-
dles that conceal the nature of the prayer.

⑤ **Festival Hats**
The circular hats worn at festivals and in *kagura* ritual
dances are brightly colored, unlike those worn for protection against the elements. Some incorporate flowers
of every month of the year.

⑥ **Yagoro-don Dolls** (Ôsumi, Kagosima Prefecture)
In a festival in November at the Iwakawa Hatiman Shrine,
a large masked figure of woven bamboo is dressed and
paraded around the village.

⑦ **Symbols of Deities**
Different forms of *hei* (paper strips on sticks) and *kezurikake* (shaved-wood objects), in which deities are believed
to reside. In the foreground are various objects used at
New Year's and the Bon Festival in August, when ancestral spirits return to earth, including treasure boats and
boats to ferry the spirits of the dead.

176

⑤ HI 2721–2798

⑥ HI 1077

⑦ HI 1008, etc.

❶ HI 0563

Japanese Houses

Traditional Japanese houses are disappearing rapidly, but their great variety of styles reflects the character of the different regions in Japan. This display presents ten representative houses in photographic panels, and four of these have been reproduced in 1/10 scale models. To make them more lifelike, the models are presented with appropriate vegetation, walls, and outbuildings, and the time is set in early November, so that the climatic variation can be understood: the trees of the *magariya* (L-shaped, "bent-house" style) house show the colors of deepening autumn in the northeastern Tôhoku region; in the mountain village of the *gassyô-zukuri* ("principal-rafter" style) house, the harvest is over and it is time to prepare for the approaching harsh winter; autumn sunlight on white walls and persimmon trees distinguish the farmhouse from the Yamato area; and the coral sand of the Okinawan house is a brilliant white, accented by flowering hibiscus and a windbreak of *hukugi* (*Garcinia subelliptica Merr.*) trees. One portion of an actual *tyûmon-zukuri* (L-shaped, "attached-gate" style) house is also shown.

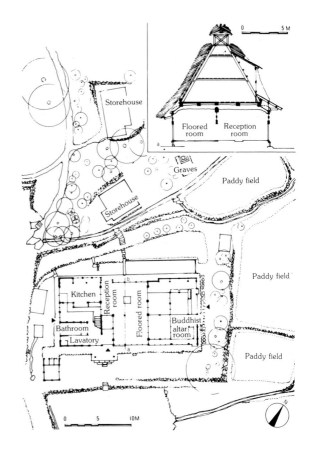

❶ Gassyô-zukuri House (1/10 scale model, floor plan and compound layout, and sectional view) (Taira, Toyama Prefecture)

This traditional style of dwelling in mountain villages of the Hida region in central Japan has a steep roof in the *gassyô-zukuri* style, which prevents snow accumulating on the roof. The floors above the first floor were used for raising silkworms, and rethatching was done cooperatively. The pond next to the house was in case of fires and for melting snow from the roof. The actual house of which this is a model is now a *minsyuku* inn.

② HI 0749

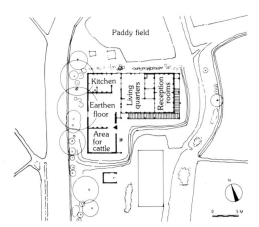

Magariya floor plan and compound layout.

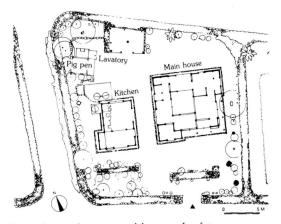

Floor plan and compound layout of a *futamune-zukuri* ("divided-ridge" style) house.

② **Magariya House** (1/10 scale model) (Tôno, Iwate Prefecture)
Such houses, which take their name and shape from the stable that juts out on one side, were common in the Nanbu area where horses were raised. Inside the stable on the left is an entrance to the house. With fewer horses today and other changes in lifestyle, the number of *magariya* has decreased sharply.

③ **Futamune-zukuri House** (1/10 scale model) (Taketomi Island, Okinawa Prefecture)
This is an old building style in which the main house and the cooking area are under separate roofs: the large thatched building is the main house, and the red-tiled building is the cooking area. To withstand typhoons, the ridge is strengthened by thatch in the former building, and in the latter the tiles are held in place by thick white plaster. The buildings are surrounded by a stone wall and a windbreak of *hukugi* trees, and a separate wall stands in front of the entrance.

③ HI 0003

❶ HI 0228

❶ **Yamato-mune House** (1/10 scale model) (Tenri, Nara Prefecture)
The gables at both ends of the main roof are covered with mud and white plaster and roofed with tiles, and they are called *takahe* (high fences) by the local people. This is the most refined of all the styles of Japanese houses, with the main house surrounded by buildings and gardens. Such compounds are common in the Nara plain, or Yamato, area.

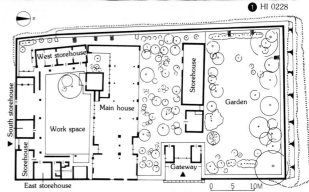

A *tyûmon-zukuri* house in a mountain village (Sakae, Nagano Prefecture).

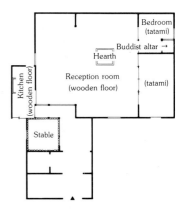

Floor plan of the Akiyama village house before it was moved.

❷–❸ **Interior of an Akiyama Village House** (section of an actual house) (Sakae, Nagano Prefecture)
Akiyama is a mountain village with heavy snowfalls. Before this house was moved, it was a *tyûmon-zukuri* building with a stable, cooking area, and hallway jutting out from the central room. *Tyûmon* refers to the part that juts out from the main house. The house has been re-

stored here to its original early nineteenth-century form. The main room has an open hearth in the center, and the walls are covered with straw. The room re-creates the evening of Little New Year, originally the night of the first full moon, now January 15. ❷ is a view of the inside of the house from the stable, which has been cut away.

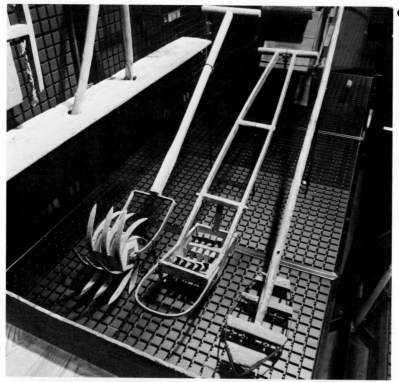

❶ HI 0240
HI 0242
HI 0243

❸ HI 0292

❹ HI 0248

❺ HI 0249

❻ HI 0247

❷ HI 0299, etc.

❼ HI 0311   ❽ HI 0270

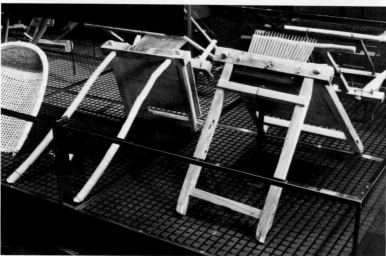

Tools from Daily Life

A variety of work tools are displayed, including some related to clothing and lifestyles. The four different displays are "Farming and Transportation Tools," "Tools for Work in the Mountains," "Clothing, Footgear, and Headwear," and "Tools from Daily Life." All the objects are now obsolete: for example, rice-harvesting tools like the reaping hook and the "thousand-toothed" thresher have been replaced by the combine, which can do everything from harvesting to threshing at one time. In the same way, hand saws have been replaced by chain and electric saws, and paper-covered standing lamps by electric lamps. Thus, machines have taken over from hand tools, causing a major upheaval in people's lives. These old tools are evocative of former lifestyles.

❶ **Weeders**
When these are pushed along between rows of rice plants, the toothed wheel turns and digs up weeds. One weeder (*right*) has fixed metal teeth instead of a toothed wheel.

❷ **Rice Threshers**
Rice stalks are placed between the teeth and pulled so that the grains fall on the far side. Rice used to be threshed stalk by stalk, but this device made it possible to thresh larger quantities at one time.

❸–❻ **Sickles**
These include grass-cutting sickles and reaping hooks, the latter with a semicircular blade that gathers the rice stalks into sheaves as they are cut. ❸ is used in the mountains.

❼–❽ **Bean Beaters** (Isigami, Iwate Prefecture)
Used to beat bean pods to extract the beans.

9 HI 0231-0233

❾ Plows and Hoes
The hoes on the wall are for preparing paddies. The plow in front was pulled by a horse.

❿ Basket (Ôsima, Tôkyô)

⓫ Back Basket (Takatiho, Miyazaki Prefecture)
Most baskets are made of strong vine or bamboo that are easy to weave, and shapes differ according to purpose.

⓬ Back Pad (Syônai, Yamagata Prefecture)
This pad, beautifully decorated with woven designs and colorful cloth, is used to carry gifts for betrothals and weddings.

⓭ Back Frames (*right*: Hirono, Yamagata Prefecture; *left*: Sannohe, Aomori Prefecture)
Used to carry objects on the back, and composed of a part that rests against the back and a three- to five-step frame.

⓮ Hulling Mill (Amami-Ôsima, Kagosima Prefecture)
Unhulled rice is poured into the upper mill (*right*) as it is turned, so the rice is ground against the ridges of the lower mill (*left*) to separate the husks from the grains.

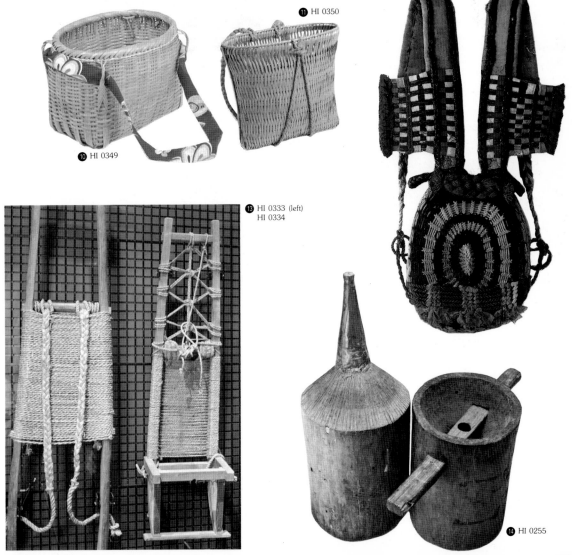

⓬ HI 0376

⓫ HI 0350

❿ HI 0349

⓭ HI 0333 (left)
HI 0334

⓮ HI 0255

183

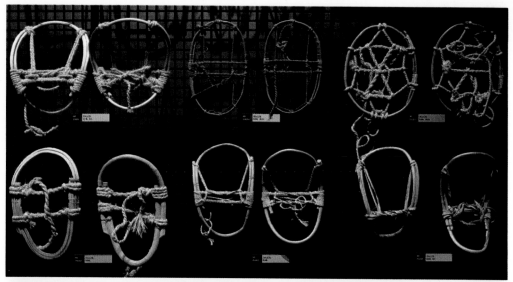

❶ HI 0450, etc.

❷ HI 0492, etc.

❶ **Snowshoes**
Tied over straw boots with rope. Oval snowshoes are for the mountains, and circular ones for flat areas.

❷ **Straw Boots and Shoes**
These straw boots were used for walking in snow because straw provides good insulation.

❸ **Saws**
There are two basic types of saw: the drawing saw (*left*) to cut parallel to the grain, used for making boards, and the crosscut saw (*right*) to cut across the grain for carpentry. Shapes differ according to use.

❹ **Sledge** (Oguti, Isikawa Prefecture)
Used for transporting logs on snow-covered hillsides. The special features are the single runner and the long poles on one side used for steering. Logs were laid between the poles.

❺ **Hunting Coat** (Sakae, Nagano Prefecture)
A coat made from the skin of a Japanese serow. It is waterproof and very warm, and snow slides off it.

❻ **Scoop** (Tabayama, Yamanasi Prefecture)
This was used for shoveling earth over charcoal so that it would keep burning after it had been removed from a charcoal kiln.

❼ **Hatchet** (Okinawa Prefecture)
This was used throughout the Ryûkyû Islands, mainly for clearing trees in the mountains. It was carried in a wooden sheath.

❽–❿ **Gunpowder Holders** (❽ Akita Prefecture; ❾ Takata, Hirosima Prefecture; ❿ Tutibuti, Iwate Prefecture)
In old-style hunting guns, gunpowder was necessary as a charge to fire the lead bullets.

③ HI 0522–
HI 0528

④ HI 0474

⑤ HI 0562

⑦ HI 0516

⑥ HI 0541

⑧ HI 0547

⑨ HI 0556

⑩ HI 0551

❶ HI 0714·0713
HI 0715·0716
HI 0717

❷ HI 0660, etc.

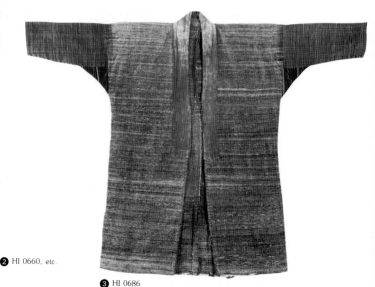

❸ HI 0686

❶ Straw Coats
People engaged in farming and other outdoor work wore these straw coats over their work clothes to keep off rain and snow and for protection against the sun.

❷ Hats
The many different shapes derived from different uses. The two hats to the right in the bottom row were designed to cover the head completely and were worn when it was snowing.

❸ Work Clothing (Sado, Niigata Prefecture)
Cloth was expensive, so old clothing was torn into narrow strips and rewoven into strong cloth.

❹ Spinning Wheel (Hurusato, Totigi Prefecture)
The spinning and twisting of thread by turning the large wheel are stages in the weaving process.

❹ HI 0676

186

⑤ HI 0693
⑥ HI 0711
⑦ HI 0709
⑧ HI 0710
⑨ HI 0696

⑤ Adjustable Pot Hanger (Suwa, Nagano Prefecture)
Used to suspend pots and tea kettles over an open hearth, the length of such pot hangers could be adjusted by varying the tension between the horizontal wooden strip and the vertical rod.

⑥, ⑧ Papered Standing Lamps and **⑦ Lantern** (**⑥, ⑧** Tôkyô; **⑦** Takesima, Kagosima Prefecture)
Such lights were in use before the advent of electricity. Originally, fish oil was used, but because of its strong smell this was replaced by rapeseed oil and candles.

⑨ Sidebati (Ogôti, Tôkyô)
Rooms were also lit by burning shredded pine roots in such stone saucers.

⑩ Basket Cradle (Niigata Prefecture)
Throughout Japan, babies slept in such baskets from birth until they could crawl.

⑪ Straw Sandals and Wooden Clogs
Some clogs have supports affixed to the bottom of the sole, while others are carved all of a piece. There are also wooden clogs for use in the snow. Some straw sandals were gripped by the toes, while others were laced around the foot.

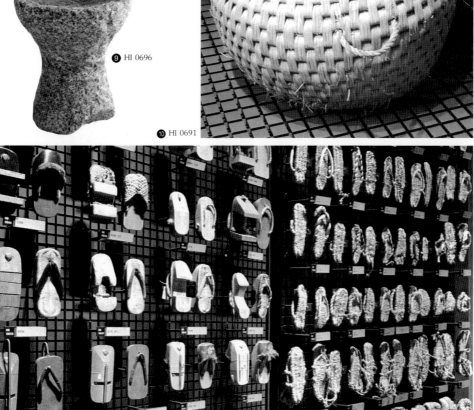

⑩ HI 0691

⑪ HI 0589
HI 0618
etc.

187

❶ HI 0754 , etc.

Crafts of Everyday Life

This exhibit includes *kokesi* dolls, eating utensils, and hand-made paper, all crafts that originated in mountain villages and were then brought to the plains. Most of the objects displayed here have disappeared from everyday life and have lost their practical value. However, the fine techniques that go into some crafts have come to be valued once again, and these objects are today produced as traditional crafts. In other words, they have survived today because their value has changed from a functional to an aesthetic one. People in every age have sought to enrich their lives by the pursuit of both beauty and utility, even in such simple tools as wooden ladles.

❶-❷ Kokesi Dolls
These dolls were originally carved by woodworkers and later became commercialized. Among the many styles are those of Naruko, Tôgatta, and Kiziyama. There are various accounts of their origins, one of which says they are representations of the *osira* deities worshiped in northeastern Japan, and another that they evolved from an infant's pacifier.

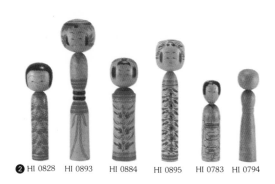

❷ HI 0828　HI 0893　HI 0884　HI 0895　HI 0783　HI 0794

❸ Ladles, Bowls, and Lunch Boxes
Wooden eating utensils were originally called *goki* and were difficult to clean, but that problem disappeared with the emergence of ceramics. The kitchen then became a place associated with cleanliness.

❹ Horned Bucket and Saké Bucket (Yokkaiti, Mie Prefecture)
Horned buckets for holding saké, often lacquered red, take their name from the long shafts resembling horns and were used at such celebrations as New Year's and weddings.

❸ HI 3504
HI 3744
HI 3652
etc.

❹ HI 3808
HI 3810

❶ Trays and Tray Tables
Over history, many distinctive woodwork techniques developed, such as hollowing out and joinery, evident in these trays and low tables.

❷ Japanese Paper-making (Uma, Ehime Prefecture)
This craft developed in mountain villages. The fibrous bark of such plants as the paper mulberry is steamed in a cauldron, the fibers removed and pulped, and the pulp placed in a large vat into which a mold is dipped to make sheets of paper.

❶ HI 3444
HI 3602, etc.

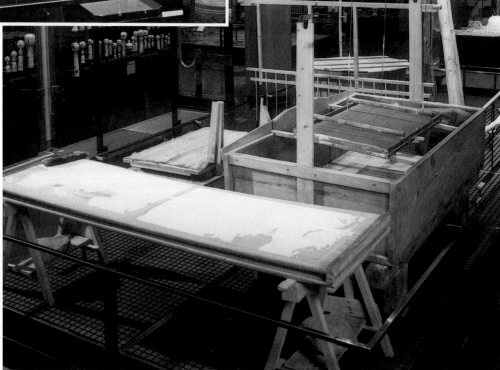

❷ HI 3841–
HI 3862

Boats and Fishing Tools

Although a fisherman may boast of his skill in handling his boat and seeking out fish, it is his tools that allow him to catch his prey. Long ago, a fisherman's hands were his tools, but when people discovered fire and learned to fashion metal, they began to use metal tools for catching fish. Before that, poles or stones were probably used, but after experimenting with more advanced tools such as fishhooks, traps, and spears, the fishermen's lives began to change substantially. With motor power, it became possible for them to fish in distant waters, and the invention of synthetic fibers increased the durability of nets and lines. The history of boats and fishing tools might be regarded as a record of the attempts of Japanese fishermen to increase their catch: since the size of the catch on any day immediately affected the household budget, a fisherman's knowledge of the seas and the habits of fish was of primary importance, as well as how well he could combine that knowledge with his skill in using his boat and tools.

❸ HI 0220
HI 4050

❹ HI 4054

❸ Octopi Pots (Awa, Tiba Prefecture)
Octopi live in deep-water crevices, and fishermen catch them by lowering ceramic pots to the ocean floor for the octopi to enter. Spearing methods are also used.
❹ Fishing Lamp (Okinawa, Okinawa Prefecture)
This lamp was used for attracting fish and was essential for night fishing, but such early lights were too weak to attract great numbers of fish.
❺ Fishing Tools
In coastal areas, longline fishing and squid fishing are predominant, and the tools show great originality. Designs for the tackle used to catch squid, such as *hikôki* (airplanes) and *hane* (wings), are especially creative.

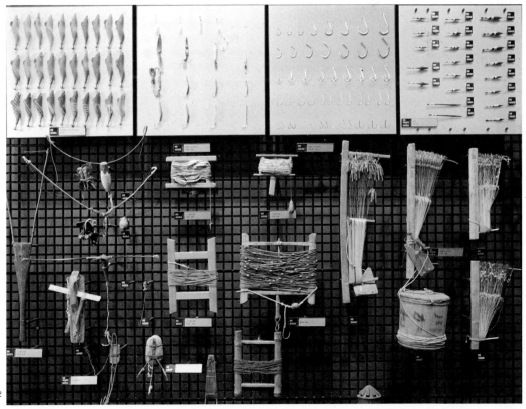

❺ HI 0042
etc.

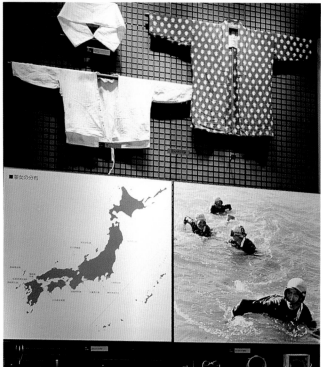

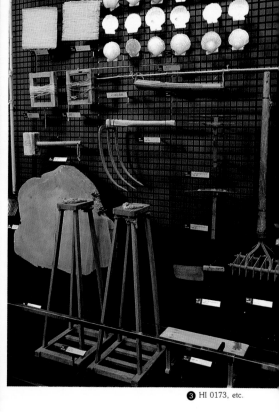

❸ HI 0173, etc.

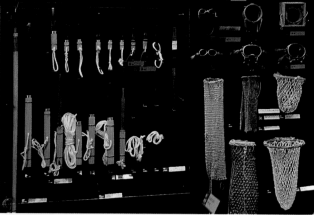

❶ HI 4105, etc.

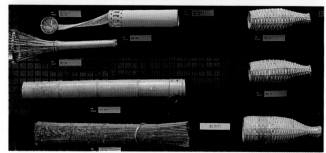

❷ HI 4001, etc.

❶ Women Divers' Tools

Today, women divers wear wet suits, but originally they wore only a skirt around their waists. Tucked into their skirt was a chisel for prising abalone from rocks, and a net bag was hung in front. Diving goggles were first used in the Meizi period (1868–1912), although divers were unable to reach any great depth with them.

❷ Fish Traps

Traps such as these were used for fishing in the shallow waters of rivers, lakes, and swamps. Their names vary according to region.

❸ Tools for Gathering Seaweed

The most unusual tool for seaweed gathering is the *tatiko-*

mi, a pair of wooden clog stilts worn when placing *hibi* (wooden or bamboo collecting boards) in the ocean. There are also many small tools, including the boards and a special knife for cutting seaweed.

❹ Yanbaru Boat (full-size replica) (Okinawa, Okinawa Prefecture)

Yanbaru boats were used to transport wood and charcoal from the northern to the southern part of the island of Okinawa. Their origins can be traced to the Edo period (1603–1867), but their shape changed greatly in the Meizi period. Unlike traditional Japanese boats, they are equipped with a keel.

④ HI 4081

The Videotheque

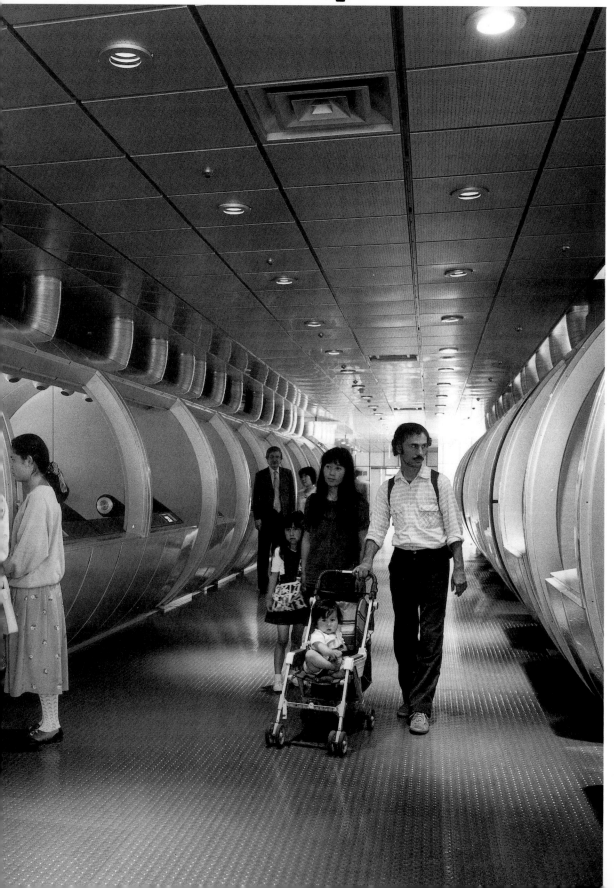

This automatic audio-visual information transmission device employs a system developed by the museum. At the touch of a button, an audio presentation and visual display is provided, showing the lifestyles of the world's many peoples, including their folk music and languages.

This device for playing videos, called the Videotheque, was created by Japanese technicians who worked with researchers at various universities to develop the basic concept of the museum's research staff. As regards ethnological museums in general, Japan lags behind many other nations in both number and types of collections, but, thanks to high technology, the Videotheque is an innovation unparalleled in the world.

Unlike television programs, over which the audience has no control, this equipment allows the visitor to choose programs freely. There is a control room, and forty viewing booths line three sides of the museum's central patio. The booths (thirty-four for two persons, six for six persons) provide a total of 104 seats. All the programs are stored in the control room on laser discs, and when the

viewer makes the selection, a robot automatically locates and loads the specified disk. The viewer in the booth calls up a program by inserting a card and touching the appropriate directions on the monitor. A color catalogue of programs with brief commentaries is provided in each booth. Each program is about ten minutes long, and at present (1991) there are about 417 programs, all complementing the artifacts on exhibition by showing how they are used in daily life and by introducing religious rites and performing arts, which cannot be conveyed by artifacts alone. The programs have all been written and produced under the careful supervision of our research staff. Since the museum opened, the Videotheque has proved extremely popular, and the list of programs will be expanded as research and the collection of artifacts proceeds.

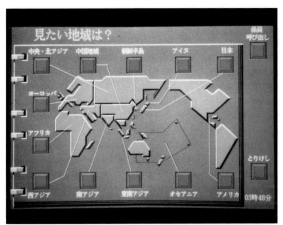

The monitor displays the regions of the world.

The Gaine, the "wandering minstrels" of the Himalayas.

One of the Videotheque booths.

Acknowledgments

MUSEUM PROJECT TEAMS, as of September 1990 (team leaders are indicated with an asterisk):

Oceania: Tomoya Akimichi, Naomichi Ishige, Shuzo Ishimori, Shuzo Koyama, Toshio Matsuyama, *Osamu Sakiyama, Ken-ichi Sudo, Hisatsugu Sugimoto, Shuji Yoshida.

The Americas: Tatsuhiko Fujii, Etsuko Kuroda, Hirochika Nakamaki, Chikasato Ogyu, *Hiroyasu Tomoeda, Norio Yamamoto, Yoshiho Yasugi.

Europe: Hiroshi Daimaru, Akiko Mori, *Masaichi Nomura, Ryo Ogawa, Chikasato Ogyu, Yasuhiro Omori, Hiroshi Shoji.

Africa: Paul K. Eguchi, Katsuyoshi Fukui, *Nobuyuki Hata, Ryo Ogawa, Kazuo Ohtsuka, Toh Sugimura, Shohei Wada, Kenji Yoshida.

West Asia: Tomoaki Fujii, Motoko Katakura, *Masatake Matsubara, Kazuo Ohtsuka, Toh Sugimura.

South Asia: Shingo Einoo, Tomoaki Fujii, *Yasuyuki Kurita, Yasuhiko Nagano.

Music: *Tomoaki Fujii, Tetsuo Sakurai.

Language: Paul K. Eguchi, Masatake Matsubara, Yasuhiko Nagano, Masaichi Nomura, Ryo Ogawa, *Osamu Sakiyama, Hiroshi Shoji, Yoshiho Yasugi.

Southeast Asia: Yukio Hayashi, Kazuko Matsuzawa, Masaru Miyamoto, Komei Sasaki, Koji Sato, Takashi Sugishima, Takuji Takemura, Katsumi Tamura, Shigeharu Tanabe, *Shuji Yoshida, Shinobu Yoshimoto.

Central and North Asia: Yuki Konagaya, Masatake Matsubara, *Kazuyoshi Ohtsuka, Shiro Sasaki, Hiroshi Shoji, Toh Sugimura.

East Asia
Korea: Toshio Asakura, *Tetsuo Sakurai, Takuji Takemura.
China: Chou Ta-Sheng, Hiroshi Daimaru, *Tomoaki Fujii, Yuki Konagaya, Masatake Matsubara, Yasuhiko Nagano, Komei Sasaki, Takuji Takemura, Shigeyuki Tsukada.
The Ainu: Masaki Kondo, *Kazuyoshi Ohtsuka, Shiro Sasaki.
Japan: Masaki Kondo, Toshio Matsuyama, *Takeshi Moriya, Hirochika Nakamaki.

JAPANESE EDITION OF THE CATALOGUE (1986)
General Supervisor: Tadao Umesao.
Chairman of the Editorial Board: Komei Sasaki.
Vice Chairman of the Editorial Board: Hisatsugu Sugimoto.
Associate Editors: Shingo Einoo; Tomoaki Fujii; Akio Hata; Nobuyuki Hata; Yoshiharu Ikeda; Shuzo Ishimori; Mikiharu Itoh; Masatake Matsubara; Takeshi Moriya; Hirochika Nakamaki; Chikasato Ogyu; Kazuo Ohtsuka; Kazuyoshi Ohtsuka; Kiyoshi Okada; Osamu Sakiyama; Tetsuo Sakurai; Takuji Takemura; Shigeharu Tanabe; Hiroyasu Tomoeda; Hidejiro Uji; Yuiti Wada; Eiko Yuasa.

Writers (square brackets indicate the person is no longer on the museum staff, as of September 1990): Tomoya Akimichi; Chou Ta-Sheng; Hiroshi Daimaru; Paul K. Eguchi; Tatsuhiko Fujii; Tomoaki Fujii; Katsuyoshi Fukui; Nobuyuki Hata; Naomichi Ishige; Shuzo Ishimori; Yuka Izumi; Motoko Katakura; [Kyuzo Kato]; [Hisako Kimishima]; [Yoshinobu Kotani]; Shuzo Koyama; Etsuko Kuroda; Masatake Matsubara; Toshio Matsuyama; Masaru Miyamoto; Takeshi Moriya; Yasuhiko Nagano; Hirochika Nakamaki; [Shunkichi Nakamura]; [Kazuyoshi Nakayama]; Ryo Ogawa; [Osamu Ogo]; Kazuo Ohtsuka; Kazuyoshi Ohtsuka; Osamu Sakiyama; Tetsuo Sakurai; Komei Sasaki; Shiro Sasaki; Mayumi Shigematsu; [Takao Sofue]; Ken-ichi Sudo; Hisatsugu Sugimoto; Toh Sugimura; Takuji Takemura; Shigeharu Tanabe; Hiroyasu Tomoeda; Shohei Wada; [Yuiti Wada]; Yoshiho Yasugi; Shuji Yoshida; Shinobu Yoshimoto.

ENGLISH EDITION OF THE CATALOGUE
General Supervisor: Tadao Umesao.
Chairman of the Editorial Board: Tomoaki Fujii.
Associate Editors: Tatsuhiko Fujii; Kazuko Matsuzawa; Koji Sato; Hiroshi Shoji; Toh Sugimura; Eiji Okude; Hidejiro Uji; Osamu Wakatsuki.

Photography by Takeshi Nishikawa, Keisuke Kumagiri, Kazunari Kuroda.
Cover design and layout by Kaneo Shimazu.

GENERAL INFORMATION

Hours: 10:00–17:00. (Admittance allowed up to 16:30.)

Closing Days: The regular closing day is Wednesday. When a national holiday falls on a Wednesday, the Museum will be closed on the following day instead. The Museum is closed from December 28 until January 4 every year. In addition, the Museum may be temporarily closed when necessary.

Address: National Museum of Ethnology
Senri Expo Park, Suita, Osaka 565, Japan.

Telephone: (06)876-2151
Facsimile: (06)875-0401

HOW TO GET TO THE MUSEUM

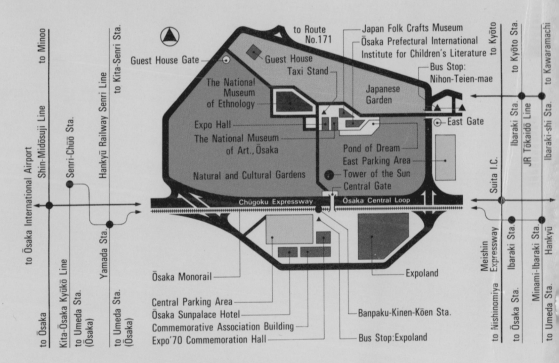

Access: Buses from JR Ibaraki Sta., Hankyū Ibaraki-shi Sta. (bound for Expoland), and Senri-Chūō Sta. (bound for Hankyū Ibaraki-shi Sta.) stop at Nihon-Teien-mae (Expo Park East Gate). From there it is about 13 minutes' walk to the Museum.

From Banpaku-Kinen-Kōen Sta. on the Ōsaka Monorail, it is about 15 minutes' walk through the Natural and Cultural Gardens to the Museum. (Please note that an admission fee is charged at the Natural and Cultural Gardens.)

Taxis are allowed to enter the National Museum of Ethnology grounds.